Nantucket Cottages and Gardens

Nantucket Cottages and Gardens

Charming Spaces on the Faraway Isle

Leslie Linsley
photography by Terry Pommett

Skyhorse Publishing

Visit our website at www.skyhorsepublishing.com.

10 9 8 7 6 5 4 3 2 1

Library of Congress Cataloging-in-Publication Data is available on file.

Cover design by Jane Sheppard
Cover photo credit: Terry Pommett

Print ISBN: 978-1-5107-1952-1
Ebook ISBN: 978-1-63450-002-9

Printed in China

Acknowledgments

Three years ago, Terry and I started a series of magazine articles for *Nantucket Today* about small houses. The idea was sparked by the awareness of a big-house building trend and we thought it was important to show how the small cottages, many built in the seventeenth and eighteenth centuries, contribute to the charm of the island. It was our intent to find a variety of houses in different parts of the island to represent the various architectural styles on Nantucket, as well as those houses with the most creative interior designs. Early into the project, we knew we had to include newly built small houses designed for modern living that fit into the landscape of the island. Visitors to Nantucket always comment on the beautiful gardens and window boxes found everywhere, even in the smallest in-town spaces. Islanders have always been passionate about their gardens, viewing them as a necessity to the quality of their lifestyles. However, one of our biggest problems was scheduling the photography during the peak summer growing time, which extended this project over several seasons.

A style book always involves many talented people without whom a project like this cannot be successful. I am most grateful to the homeowners who let us into their homes, sometimes just before or after an unexpected onslaught of guests, as often happens in the summer on Nantucket. They gave freely of their time and graciously let us move things around and disrupt their daily lives to show off their homes in the best possible light. All who contributed to making this an exciting project demonstrate how to make a small home unique and interesting by embracing its size. I am fortunate to live in a community of generous friends and neighbors who never hesitate when asked to open their homes to me: Mellie and Jim Cooper were the best neighbors for many years, affording me a front row seat during the exquisite restoration of their 1800s house. I have the highest regard for Mellie's taste and, when she recommends a photo-worthy home for a book or magazine project, she is always spot-on. My other neighbors, Jean Doyen de Montaillou and his life partner, Michael Kovner, are the most generous homeowners, going the extra mile to style their home and help make a photo shoot a memorable experience. This is their second home to be included in one of my books. Around the corner, Ginny Kinney's talented craftsmanship is a testament to her creative lifestyle. I appreciate Ed and Joan Lahey, who, fortunately for me, sold their large home after we included it in our book, *Nantucket Island Living,* and then downsized to a cottage they restored in time to include in this book. Their respectful restoration is admirable. Interior designer Margo Montgomery introduced me to Susan Sandler, whose kitchen she designed, and interior designer Kathleen Hay, who always goes out of her way to point me in the right direction. Designer Trudy Dujardin, along with her colleague Price Connor, and writer Lisa Clair, have provided me with consummate Nantucket style homes to photograph for many years.

Reggie Levine, Lyn Walsh, Peter Greenhalgh, Stacey Stuart, Donn Russell, and Greg and Judy Hill are part of the Nantucket art scene. Their homes are a testament to their devotion to keeping history alive by surrounding themselves with family heirlooms and supporting local artists. Thank you to Jeremy and Patricia David, Ann and Van Smith, the Rose family, Deborah Hohlt, and Mary Beth and Barnard Barrett, who opened their homes to us and let us do our thing even when it meant rearranging furniture. Thanks go to contractor Jay Hanley for his thoughtful advice and tips on building your own small home. His shipshape "bachelor pad" is a wonderful example of function and good design.

There were more gardens than we could possibly include, but we are especially grateful to have captured the exceptional gardens of Ian and Carolyn McKenzie, Prentice and Patricia Claflin, and to introduce the unusual concept of a "rill" through Connie Umberger's in-town garden.

'Sconset is a world apart from downtown Nantucket, and being in the village for several days shooting the earliest cottages and gardens on the island was beyond magical. We owe a huge bouquet of garden roses to Michael May and Housley Carr; Mary Williams, an incredibly talented and respectful restorer of early cottages; Deb and Angus McCloed, who helped us in so many ways including plying us with the best egg salad sandwiches during a long shoot; and Ed Daisey and Ginny Hill Daisey, whose home I originally included in my book, *Nantucket Style,* in 1992. Ginny's devotion to the details of reinventing the perfect cottage garden is unparalleled and it was such fun to revisit this home and find it as welcoming filled with grandchildren as it was when their parents were the children. Now, as then, they were in and out of the house throughout the entire photo shoot.

Thank you Pete Smith and Hillary Newell from Bartlett's Oceanview Farm and Greg Beni of Surfing Hydrangea Nursery for tips on growing hydrangeas and to Carole Fauth for the perfect cottage in Key West where I did my final editing away from the hustle and bustle of Nantucket in August.

The experience of editing the book was positively joyful due to my editor, Nicole Frail, as well as my respect for Skyhorse Publishing's designers, who worked with my graphic designer husband, Jon Aron, on the design of the book. My agent of many years, Linda Konner, always works tirelessly on my behalf and without her this project would not have been possible. I owe her my greatest respect.

Finally, I want to thank Marianne Stanton, publisher of the *Nantucket Inquirer & Mirror* and *Nantucket Today* magazine for the opportunity to be part of a contributing team of talented professionals for more than thirty years. I am passionate about Nantucket Island and our community and can't think of a better way to earn a living than writing about it.

—*Leslie Linsley*

If you're inspired to make your own Nantucket cottage style projects as seen throughout the book, go to my website for patterns: leslielinsley.com.

TABLE OF CONTENTS

A rose-covered cottage in the village of 'Sconset.

INTRODUCTION

When I was a little girl and first came to Nantucket Island with my parents, we always rented little cottages. Often, the cottages were near or right on the beach and they were always rustic, much like typical summer cabins. Throughout the years, these basic little cottages disappeared to make way for larger, more luxurious homes, but many of us are nostalgic for these simple structures that represented carefree summer living. At that time my mother would say, "My dream house is one in which you simply sweep the sand out the front door at the end of the day." She called it her "selfish little house." After college, I sold my first book and used the money to buy that little selfish cottage in the Historic District of Nantucket where I have lived ever since. The cottage has expanded over the years, but it still has the ephemeral qualities of the original. An unpretentious cottage is as much a state of mind as a destination—a place where a family can enjoy a simple way of living.

Nantucket Island is a spit of land, seven miles wide and fourteen miles long, located thirty miles off the coast of Cape Cod in Massachusetts. It can only be reached by boat or plane, but has a year-round population of twelve thousand. Everywhere you look, you see evidence of Nantucket's rich history as a thriving whaling community where men went off to sea for months at a time. Today, the island boasts more than 1,200 structures built in the 1800s, though some date back to the 1600s and 1700s. More than eight hundred houses were built on the island before the Civil War. The Nantucket Preservation Trust (NPT) is an organization that strives to preserve Nantucket's architectural heritage. Through educational tours, publications, and slide shows, the NPT works to enlighten the public about the significance of preserving both the exteriors and interiors of the island's historic architecture, as well as its gardens and streetscapes.

Though Nantucket is rooted in its rich history, it is really the relationship between its historical past and current influences that characterizes the island's appealing style, whether in interior design, arts and crafts, or gardens.

Nowhere in this country are there more charming and diverse cottages featuring small pocket gardens and window boxes than on Nantucket Island. And now many of these cottages are being renovated by responsible homeowners, designers, and artisans for modern-day living without losing their original appeal. There is something incredibly humbling about these cottages that take you back to a gentler time, and it makes you realize it might be achievable today.

Walk down any street or lane on the island and you will find a darling cottage tucked neatly between two large family homes or in back of another. To a large extent, the character of the island is reflective of these little early homes. They were originally built by and for island residents at a time when some people—those who lived in them—didn't require, didn't desire, or couldn't afford anything larger. These houses contribute to the island's diversity, something we are coming dangerously close to losing as larger, newer homes nudge them out of the way or simply overshadow them.

Small houses are also being built from scratch in the style of these early Nantucket cottages, so they fit into the landscape of the island. Others are being built with architectural details borrowed from larger, historic homes in the Historic District and reinterpreted for scaled-down living. Simple living is a precious commodity, especially when surrounded by the natural beauty of the island.

Probably, the most charming of all the early cottages are the whale cottages in the village of Siasconset at the eastern end of the island. The name derived from the Native American *Missiaskonset* for "near the great whale." Originally built as fishing shacks or for lodging a six-man boat crew in very cramped quarters, these structures were later used as summer homes by people who wanted a simple existence, if only for a few weeks. Many of these little cottages have remained in the same families for generations. They appreciate the quaintness of the places, with the yards in front of each house delineated by a picket fence and pocket gardens. However, while some of these cottages are left just as they were in the 1700s as a tribute to Nantucket history, others have been updated on the interiors for year-round living and are equally charming with the added appeal of modern amenities.

Then there are the beach cottages. Nothing conjures up romance and a feeling of freedom quite like the image of a small, simple cottage with only beach grasses and sand dunes between its occupants and the water.

Nantucket residents are passionate about their gardens. Some are small, in-town, pocket gardens, others are border gardens seen along picket fences. Some are formal, others more uninhibited, depending on the site and the gardener. But the most charming gardens all over the island are those resembling a typical cottage garden that looks as though it just grew up on its own, a little jaunty and carefree.

But even at a time when modern techniques and taste in home furnishings change with each new influx of homeowners, the classic design elements of cottage style have survived on Nantucket. Our community is composed of a diversity that has evolved through interaction and amalgamation from all over the world. We have become a sophisticated bunch with an inherent ability to recognize quality goods. We have a broad base of input and a history of appreciation for fine things. This is one of the reasons that Nantucket has attracted some of the country's most talented artisans.

This is the second book about Nantucket Island living that Terry and I have worked on together; however, we also produce a dozen magazine articles each year featuring Nantucket homes and the lifestyle of the people who own them. We are often asked if we're bothered by the inevitable changes on the island. We are more than familiar with the island's growth. Having lived here for more than forty years, we are both acutely aware that gentrification, found in so many resort areas, has been a main source of concern on Nantucket. But the prevailing attitude is accepting of any number of diverse factions. It is this diversity of opinion that makes up the fabric of the island and encourages lively conversation among the locals. Much good has come out of the changes to the island in the form of improved services and the economy in general. Many historic houses have been reclaimed and, fortunately, have passed into the hands of people with taste and imagination and the means and awareness to restore and adapt them for current use without destroying their history.

I have always been fascinated by the early island cottages and the fact that they have survived. While working on this book, we became immersed in the way people live in small homes. After a day's shoot, we often came away with ideas for our own homes. Some of the early cottages, with their uneven floors, while charming, often gave us vertigo and we laughed about how it felt much like living on a boat. Sometimes that was the idea. The newly built cottages were amazingly designed—they fit the landscape of the island and had exquisite interior designs featuring furnishings from around the world, much like the early Nantucket sea captains' homes, which were furnished with the fine goods brought back from their travels to Europe, Africa, and Asia. The abundance and quality of Chinese artifacts in the Nantucket Historical Association's outstanding and diverse collection indicates the level of island involvement in the China trade. Things aren't much different today. Even the small houses are filled with beautiful objects, some from the island and many brought here from travels around the world. Islanders have a passion for their homes, whether they own a grand mansion overlooking the ocean or a tiny one-room cottage tucked down an in-town lane.

Living small, as typified by cottage living, has become a responsible, chic, innovative, and practical wave of the immediate future, not only on Nantucket, but throughout the country. Many homeowners are rethinking their needs in regard to space, opting for more quality and less quantity of square footage.

A small home is one that can be infused with special details and designed to accommodate the lifestyle of its occupants. Neither size nor volume has anything to do with style and comfort. Perhaps the cottages of Nantucket will inspire those who are building new, renovating, or decorating a small home.

The small house concept works when superfluous square footage is traded for less tangible, but more meaningful, aspects of design. Window seats, built-ins, natural woodwork, bookcases, efficient kitchen appliances, and attention to details add quality to the use of the rooms. Sprinkled throughout the book, you'll find creative ways to solve small house problems that are just as helpful for those living in larger homes. Many homeowners have interesting ideas for storage. A gallery owner demonstrates an interesting way to arrange collections and hang art, another extolls the virtue of living with family heirlooms, some have downsized elegantly and others are particularly adept at entertaining with style. You'll see how architects, designers, builders, and homeowners have responsibly built, restored, renovated, and decorated with fresh approaches.

These cottages are not isolated even if they are far removed from another dwelling. Whether a cottage looks out over the ocean, was built in a private country setting, is practically touching another cottage on either side, or is hidden at the end of an in-town lane, they have one thing in common and that is the island itself. The people who live in these cottages and tend to their gardens are ever mindful of the natural beauty and the history of Nantucket and how it impacts the way we live.

Decorating with a Nantucket Cottage Style

Any home, no matter its style, can be infused with a little bit of Nantucket cottage elements for comfort, character, and charm. The enduring interiors are often under-decorated ones, where the owners were more concerned with being themselves than trying to create a look. (The Nantucket Historical Association in conjunction with the Artists Association of Nantucket featured an exhibit called "Nantucket Cottage Style" in the historic Whaling Museum on Broad Street.)

The following will define some of the classic elements of furnishing your home with Nantucket cottage style:

1. *Pastel or white interior paint scheme along with plain wooden floors and open ceilings.*
2. *Painted or scrub pine furniture and weathered wood tables. Even if you have a modern home, or have furnished with more up-to-date furnishings, adding a piece or two from the past will always give a room character.*
3. *Handmade textiles in muted earth tones and fabrics in stripes as per Swedish country style are timeless.*
4. *Solid fabrics in garden green or seaside blue will never ever go out of style on Nantucket or elsewhere.*
5. *Natural fiber rugs such as sisal are perfectly lovely over painted wooden floors.*
6. *Quilted bed covers and braided rugs were a mainstay of Jacqueline Kennedy Onasis's private quarters at the White House. Her decorator, the famous Sister Parish of Hadley Parish Design was responsible for introducing her to this comfortably homey style, and Jackie often shopped for these items on Nantucket.*
7. *Objects of art such as pottery, earthenware, antique tins, wooden grain scoops and boxes, furniture painted with milk paint, oil lamps, bird decoys, boat models, lightship baskets, and scrimshaw—these are the handcrafts most often identified with Nantucket. Local artwork is a big part of Nantucket cottage style.*
8. *In the summertime, we think of carefree. No one wants to live with fussy things that need lots of maintenance. There is nothing more inviting and cottage style than a bouquet of wildflowers—not a styled bouquet, but one that is fresh picked and uninhibited. Dried flowers hanging from a rafter are also lovely.*
9. *Seashells along a window ledge are so simple in colors and shapes, and beach towels rolled up in floor baskets are a mainstay of cottage casual, suggesting an unpretentious lifestyle.*
10. *Art books and books of the island piled everywhere for a spontaneous read, but also as a design element. Create a tablescape with books and art objects. Keep a pile on a small stool or child-size painted chair.*
11. *Open windows for fresh air. Create a comfortable ambience that exudes a desire to kick off one's shoes.*

A good rule of thumb: If it needs a lot of care, if it doesn't look right, if it makes you uncomfortable, if it's "wrong" but you don't know why, toss it. Nantucket cottage style is all about feeling good in your own home. It should be a peaceful oasis, like the island itself.

In-Town Cottages

The little Quaker house, located on one of Nantucket's most historic in-town byways, has been meticulously restored beyond its humble beginnings. The roof walk addition is accessed by a ladder from the upstairs hallway. It affords a view of Nantucket Harbor.

Paper parasols are fanciful decorations on the back porch and patio. Roses grow up the side of the house all summer. Hydrangeas, clematis, and Queen Anne's lace fill the garden at the back porch entryway.

An Early Gem

The size of this house, originally built in 1830, is what attracted the owners to buy and restore it. There was an old kitchen with its early porcelain sink, tilting cabinets, and old appliances, two tiny bedrooms with slanting ceilings often found in early one-and-a-half-story homes. While still charming and small, it has been restored way beyond its humble beginnings.

One of the owners, an artist, brought her artistic sensibilities to this project and carefully chose just the right furnishings, accessories, and soft, historic paint colors. "I look at every part of a room as if it is a painting," she said of her arrangements and vignettes. "I like small, intimate spaces—a house that wraps its arms around you," she added. "A small house doesn't swallow things. You can afford to have nice things and, best of all, you know where they are," she continued.

The architectural beauty of the interior is evident in the worn, patinaed, wide pine floorboards, doorways with transom, and paneled walls, accentuating rather than ignoring the simple characteristics of its Quaker roots.

The house is a typical layout for the period in which it was built, with a small entry and a stairway directly in line with the front door. A hallway runs down one side to the back of the house and to the left is a small living room. Behind that is a sitting room of the same size. There is a back-to-back fireplace in both of these rooms, which was typically the original source of heat.

As a consummate treasure hunter, the artist/owner knew how to zero in on what was really worth owning. "I look for great stuff at great prices everywhere I go and combine flea-market finds with interesting, unusual antiques. When you live small, you have to love everything you put in your rooms. The things I bought for the house don't necessarily have provenance, but they have to be stylish, with some wonderful detail that makes a piece interesting," she said. "I love symmetry and when I arrange the furniture, I lean in that direction."

She says she likes all the rooms lit at night so the entire house becomes an integral part of life and then added, "With a large house, you can often live in just parts of it, never lighting all the rooms at once. It's easy to arrange pretty things and perfect your environment when your house is small. It's harder to keep track of things in larger spaces. Grouping makes a stronger statement and your rooms will be more dramatic."

It is an ongoing editing challenge. "I don't think I would have the time or the ability to find just the right eclectic, idiosyncratic items that I particularly like to fill a big house in a lifetime," she says.

The dining area, an extension of the kitchen, is a small square room. It has windows on all sides, much like a summer porch, and looks out over the garden.
The walls and ceiling are covered with fir and three different shades of green stain were used on the walls, windows, and moldings. The table is set with favorite milk glass pieces. A chandelier is more interesting than recessed lighting.

Tips for Entertaining in a Small House

1. Have drinks outside and leave the cleanup until the party is over, that way you won't have clutter in the kitchen. In cold weather, leave everything in the living room until later.

2. Use two tables in different parts of the house. Set a buffet in the kitchen and this becomes the unifying space.

3. A drop-leaf table is very practical.

4. A round dining table is preferable for a small room. There are no sharp edges to maneuver around and it promotes conversation.

5. Even if your space is small and informal, pull out all the stops when setting the table. Use your favorite things.

6. When your dining area is small, don't skimp on the aesthetics. Add things that make it elegant so that a casual, informal space used for breakfast is elegant for dinner parties.

7. Lighting in the dining room should be adjustable. Add small table lamps.

8. Choose wall art that is attractive from every angle so no matter where you are seated, you have an interesting view.

9. Plant outdoor plantings indoors.

10. Keep window treatments simple.

The new kitchen is slightly smaller than the original, allowing for built-ins and closet space, rather than a bank of cabinets along the right wall. The butcher block island serves as a buffet center. Lamps and vases on the windowsill came from Janis Aldridge Gallery on Washington Street.

Visitors arrive from the driveway through a natural archway of greenery, up a little stone path to the pocket garden and patio. A lush hedge creates privacy around this in-town property.

The living room (or front parlor, as it was called) is furnished with bamboo furniture, upholstered slipper chairs, a hooked rug, and carefully arranged accessories. The owner/artist painted the pale green stripes on the walls and the scalloped wooden window valances were custom-made.

The narrow hallway runs from the front door to the kitchen along the side of the house. The soft green stain is used throughout and the wide pine floors are the originals from the early 1800s.

A narrow hallway at the top of the stairs provides a small office area. The painting on the wall is by Mellie Cooper. The rocking horse is an antique.

The new master bedroom was designed with built-in shelves and dressers on either side of a window seat and made of the same fir used in the kitchen renovation. The painting on the wall is by Nantucket artist Robert McKee.

A back garden off the deck is brimming in late spring and summer.
Typical cottage gardens mix flowers and herbs packed tightly together.

This cottage was built to resemble an early 1800 Greek Revival and, because of its elevation, looks larger than its twenty-two by thirty-foot size. Lots of windows and an open floor plan make the interior of this one-bedroom abode light and airy.

Built for One

Most people who live in small homes say, "You simply can't waste space on anything that isn't useful, comfortable, or visually pleasing." This is how Virginia Kinney, a year-round homeowner, designed, built, and furnished her big little house. "I love old stuff, but I also love comfort. It's a practical balance. I need to be comfortable wherever I am in the house," says Kinney.

It was a small lot with a dilapidated barn on it. The barn was removed and the house was designed on the same footprint, which is only about twenty-two by thirty feet. Ginny, as she is known, had always admired the early Greek Revival houses built on the island around the mid-1800s. The houses in this part of town are some of the earliest built here, so the house was designed to fit in with the neighborhood. As a consummate do-it-yourselfer, Kinney needed a full basement to accommodate all of her projects. She also did a lot of the interior finishing work, like window trims, the built-in bookcase, and collection niche. But her real talent is in the details. She has a good eye for knowing what works well together and how to infuse the new space with character by using reclaimed materials. For example, old shutters, discarded from a house in town, with their original gray/blue paint color intact, were retrofitted for the living room windows. A handmade door with tiny handcrafted window panes and peeling paint leads from the kitchen to the basement, adding just the right amount of unexpected quirkiness to the place. It came from the local landfill.

The basement has full windows in the front, making the entrance to the house a full story above street level and affording a certain amount of privacy. Situated on a slight incline, the back of the house opens onto a deck and pocket garden all at the first floor level. The house is two stories of living space with an open kitchen, living and dining area, a hallway, walk-in closet, and full bath on the first floor. There's a second floor loft-like bedroom with built-in bookcases, plenty of under-the-eaves storage, and a feeling of spaciousness derived from a simple railing overlooking the living room, rather than a closed-in wall. "When you live alone, privacy isn't a factor to consider," Kinney says.

The furnishings combine authentic antiques with well-designed and reasonably priced reproductions. Architectural details found in early American homes, such as the decorative finishing molding at the corner of the window trims, were easier than mitering the corners and making the trim fit perfectly. Beadboard was chosen for the kitchen ceiling as well as the front of the cabinets. Not wanting to open the front door right into the living space, Kinney created a narrow entryway with a wall that doesn't quite go all the way to the ceiling. Light from the transoms in the front door spills into the kitchen on the other side of the wall.

Tips for Furnishing Your Small House

1. *The largest pieces, like sofa and chairs, should be light in color so they don't seem larger than they are, dominating the room.*
2. *Group collections together according to color, size, texture, and shape rather than scattering about. This will dramatize a collection and make a statement of importance even when mixing old and new.*
3. *Don't hesitate to buy a reproduction of an antique item if it is well-designed and reasonably priced. When mixed with a good antique, the repro will be elevated to its status.*
4. *A small house must be light and airy. When building from scratch, plan window placement for maximum natural light. You can always create privacy with shutters, shades, or curtains.*
5. *Cover windows that are too high to reach with slat blinds with extra long strings for adjusting from below.*
6. *If the floor plan is an open one, use one color throughout, preferably a light shade. You can always add color in the furnishings and artwork.*
7. *Keep your bathroom and kitchen streamlined. Find or plan clever storage tricks under the sink inside the cupboards.*
8. *A vase of cut garden flowers is the loveliest accessory on any table. An herb plant like lavender or a bowl of lemons adds a fresh scent to the room.*
9. *Everything should be in scale and simple. Try not to leave stuff on the floor.*

A drop leaf table from the owner's family home in Ohio is surrounded by good reproduction wrought iron Windsor chairs. High, small windows allow light to fill the room without sacrificing privacy. The house is tastefully appointed with the work of local artists.

A cupboard niche was built into the living room wall to house a collection of red transferware, tramp art, mosaic memory pots (some old, some created by the owner), and white ironstone. The homeowner calls this "controlled clutter." A bookcase was built in the narrow landing space upstairs. Storage is under the curtained eave. The rustic door leading to the basement came from the local landfill.

A reclaimed shelf above the stove is used to display a collection of ironstone pitchers and the cutout wall provides light from the front door leading into the entryway on the other side. An original oil painting and an old botanical print balance the display of tole trays on the wall to the right.

A loft bedroom is open to the living room below, making it feel spacious yet private. Compact office space was eked out to the right of the banister leading around to the bookcase. Everything is contained in files on wheels that can be concealed under an antique library table used as a desk.

A display of white ironstone pitchers lines the shelf of this cutout wall area and can be seen from both sides. The hallway is painted gold, one of three typical Colonial colors used throughout the house: red, gold, and black against shades of beige.

The living room to the left of the entryway is painted hydrangea blue with pure white ceilings and trim. Large mirrors in silver frames visually expand and brighten a small room and antiques are mixed with inexpensive accessories for comfort and style.

Half Union

This little cottage was originally built circa 1950s. It belonged to one family and remained unchanged for almost fifty years until Connecticut designer Jean Doyen de Montaillou reclaimed it as a guest cottage and office. Nothing structural was changed, but the interior decorations gave it up-to-date elegance, comfort, and style. The rooms are small, ceilings are low, and a narrow staircase leads to a second floor where one must duck down to enter the bedrooms on either sides of the landing. The kitchen is ample, open to a dining/sitting area. No granite countertops or Sub-Zero refrigerators here.

Jean says, "Decorating a little cottage can be liberating. You don't have to take it too seriously. You can have fun with it." Unlike many who feel the need to "unclutter," this decorator believes that a cottage can take a lot of accessories because it should be as visually interesting and physically comfortable as possible. A small cottage is the perfect blank canvas for an unexpectedly elegant approach. When you mix in a few good pieces, like an antique or two, it elevates the overall feeling. This is not, after all, a beach cottage, but an in-town home nestled among grand historic homes.

"Nothing in the house is precious or overly expensive," Jean says. "In fact most of the furnishings came from auctions and yard sales that I painted or recovered." The living room, dining, sitting, and kitchen areas are painted hydrangea blue to match the color of the hydrangeas that grow on the property. (This is one of Benjamin Moore's historical antique colors.) Using one color throughout unifies the rooms so they flow from one to the other. The front hallway and the only downstairs bedroom were painted off-white to create separation from the rest of the cottage. All the window and wall moldings were given a fresh coat of semigloss white paint.

A cottage should be maintenance-free and, toward that end, stain-resistant fabric was used on the upholstered furniture. Ready-made toile curtains reflect a pattern in the accessories such as plates, lamps, and stools (all inexpensive and easily replaced should a guest accidentally break something).

"I used lots of silver and mirrors for light and sparkle," Jean explains. "I found gold framed mirrors and painted them silver because gold is a bit heavy and too formal, while silver is more youthful. To make the living room seem larger, I placed oversized mirrors in the middle of the walls." The original hardwood floors were refinished and remain bare, allowing the soft patina of the wood to become an integral part of the design.

Tips for Decorating Small

1. *Your walls will appear taller if the ceiling is white and the walls are a color.*
2. *Molding and window trims should be the same color as the ceiling. Some decorators like to use the same color for molding and walls, sometimes making one a slightly darker shade than the other.*
3. *Don't pretend the house is larger than it is. Embrace the positive cottage quality and make it intimate.*
4. *Give your home personality that reflects who you are; for example, the collection of Tony Sarg prints framed and arranged all together on one wall in the dining area of this home.*
5. *Make a statement with a collection. For example, an arrangement of plates used as visual room dividers on a narrow wall between the kitchen and dining areas. Books and framed photographs make a small home personal. A bookcase is too heavy; pile them on a chair or coffee table. Use oversized mirrors on a wall to create a feeling of space.*
6. *On a narrow stairway, consider botanical prints in mirrored frames. Or hang a group of small, framed mirrors on a stairway wall.*
7. *Always carpet a narrow stairway with a runner, never end to end. Leave wood showing on both sides to make the stairs seem wider.*
8. *Buy the comfortable pieces first to anchor the living room. Then add smaller pieces like occasional chairs, side tables, and accessories.*
9. *Make window treatments casual but elegant. Shutters work in some cottages, but they are decidedly "cottagy." Fabric softens the windows and adds to the overall feeling of comfort and elegance.*
10. *Mix a few really good pieces with yard sale finds; for example, rush-seat dining chairs are antiques and have been outfitted with seat cushions to match the curtains. However, the table is one of no particular value, but has good lines, is sturdy, and, when given a coat of glossy paint, is the perfect complement.*

The dining area was painted with the same blue color as the fabric for the curtains and chair cushions. The owner painted the farm table and surrounded it with antique chairs. A collection of plates on a narrow wall creates a visual separation between this room and the open kitchen. Tony Sarg prints fill the wall.

The front door opens into a small entryway where a narrow staircase leads up to two second-floor bedrooms. The painted stairs are covered with a durable sisal runner, and a series of botanicals in mirrored frames give the illusion of a wider stairway.

The downstairs bedroom is painted white and continues the blue-and-white theme with touches of yellow. While small, it is sumptuously appointed with everything needed to make guests welcome: two end tables, matching lamps on either sides of the bed, plenty of pillows, and a painted highboy complete the room.

The interior design office is at the back of the house in what was once a one-room apartment. The stairway leads to a small bedroom under the eaves. The hardwood floors are original to the house and were simply sanded and finished with polyurethane.

A compact bathroom off the office was refinished with a teak ceiling to look like the inside of a ship. A star mirror on the beadboard door, half hulls, and rope knots above the doorway further reflect a nautical theme.

This 1800s cottage at the foot of Sunset Hill is surrounded with flowers.

Sunset Hill

This little cottage, built in the 1800s at the corner of Sunset Hill and North Liberty Street, was once a barrel-making shed that received additions from the next owner, a ship's carpenter. It has two chimneys on each end. Sunset Hill is best known as the location of the oldest house on the island at the top of the hill.

The elegance of compactness is evident in the approximately 750 square feet of interior space; the entire cottage comprises only four rooms. While the kitchen and bathroom have been upgraded, the original building has not been compromised in any way. The kitchen is a marvel of design, incorporating a breakfast area that doubles as a prep counter for meals and endless cubbies and shelves on even the narrowest wall. There's nothing in plain sight that could possibly suggest clutter.

The bathroom, too, has been refitted with hexagonal white tiles and modern fixtures without expanding the space that would have taken away from the two bedrooms on either side. Because the ceiling is open to the rafters and the entire interior has been painted white, the rooms do not feel cramped. Another reason for this is that the owners keep their possessions to a minimum. "Because this is our vacation home," they emphasize, "it's easy to minimize what we can bring with us from our New York City apartment when we spend three months here."

The owner says, "A small house keeps you honest. You can't be pretentious. The house speaks for itself and anything that is out of place is at once obviously 'wrong.' You have to be very clear about what you can live without and what is essential. It's hard to choose what stays and what goes. You can't be sentimental about things or they will drown you. It's important to be clear about why something is occupying the space when space is at a premium."

Tips for Clutter-Free Decorating

1. All white linens and towels add to the overall calm feeling created in a small bathroom.
2. Keep all surfaces clean. Once you get used to putting things away, throwing away papers after they are read, sorting and filing mail, etc., it becomes routine and a very good way to allow the good bones of a small home to be appreciated.
3. Think of your small home as a nest. You can make it cozy by choosing wisely so it doesn't feel cramped.
4. If you have too many things, try taking away just one thing from one area every day until you have it right.
5. In the kitchen, all one needs is a lovely bowl of fresh fruit.

Flowers grow in abundance all around the property; day lilies, tiger lilies, and hydrangeas bloom all summer long. Lavender, herbs, and flowering plants line the sweet garden path and give off lovely scents. Bright blue and pink hydrangea bushes rim the fence around the property.

The front door opens into the living room, one of four rooms in the cottage. Many of the furniture pieces were in the house when it was purchased in the 1960s; other items were bought on Nantucket.

The bathroom was updated with new fixtures and tiles on the floor. The pewter light fixture was made to scale. Straw baskets hold towels and bathroom essentials in a corner cupboard.

Island decorator Margot Montgomery designed the new kitchen with all sorts of hidden cubbies and shelves for efficiency and maximum storage. The pine-covered walls and floors are finished with a white satin stain.

A narrow shelf runs around the bedroom to hold displays. To provide efficient workspace for the owner/screenwriter, architect Sophie Metz custom-designed the built-in desk. A vintage floral appliqué quilt adds a touch of color to the all-white room.

This small plot of land is filled to brimming with well-planned vegetation that has evolved over time. A stone patio is surrounded by potted plants and bushes, statuaries, and mature trees.

World of Art

Small spaces do not inhibit collectors from collecting whatever it is they are passionate about. But, when someone with a keen eye and a good sense of space and design assembles a collection of artwork, it forms the basis of a personal environment that is both pleasing to the homeowner as well as those who visit. Former art gallery owner, artist, trained curator, and longtime Nantucket resident Reggie Levine has done just that, and the result is quite dramatic. The art defines the interior.

This house, a warren of small connecting rooms, was built in 1945 and is conveniently located on a busy road leading in and out of town. But, once inside, the world outside disappears. Even the enchanting garden at the back of the house seems far from the bustle of town.

The dominating artwork in each small room leads seamlessly into the next, creating a fascinating interior space. The paintings, antiques, and objects of art are from travels around the world. Every item has a backstory and relates artistically to those around it. All the colors of the paintings and three-dimentional objects are made of warm earth tones. Even the worn wooden floors are covered with Oriental and Persian scatter rugs in patterns and shades of the same colors.

The small entryway to the house is the first clue to what lies ahead. The kitchen to the right is just as crammed with interesting artifacts as the small dining room to the left, through which one enters the rest of the house. A large, open living space is cathedral height with a massive stone fireplace dominating one end of the room.

The house is filled with the work of every known name in the Nantucket art world, some internationally recognized, many getting their start at Reggie's former Main Street Gallery: Pierro Fenchi pottery; Paul La Paglia oils; paintings by Sherry Wilson Rae, Sterling Mulbry, Robert Perrin, Charlotte Kimble, Richard Kemble, Penny Sheerer, Andrew Shunney, and Roy Bailey to name a few.

Tips for Hanging and Arranging Artwork

1. *Consider the space where your artwork will be displayed. Consider the table or shelves where things will be arranged.*

2. *Assemble the items and consider all the elements of size, shape, etc., to create an interesting mix.*

3. *Paintings need breathing room, but you also want them to work with the surrounding items. Trust your eye.*

4. *Many galleries and museums follow the fifty-seven-inch on center standard, which represents the average human eye height. Measure up fifty-seven inches from the floor.*

5. *This fifty-seven-inch rule also applies to groups of pictures. Think of a group as one picture. After you arrange them on the floor, start with the center picture/ pictures and get them at fifty-seven inches on center. Then surround them with the rest of the group.*

6. *Use picture hanging hooks, not nails.*

7. *Use two picture hooks per artwork to keep them level over time.*

8. *Recruit a helper who can hold pieces against the wall before you hammer in the picture hooks.*

9. *When hanging a pair of works, one above the other, treat them as one large picture (whether they're the same or different sizes). Find the center point between them, and use the same fifty-seven-inch rule for the center of the combined grouping.*

10. *If you hang something and want to move it, it's really easy to fix the problem with a little spackle to fill the hole.*

11. *For three-dimensional objects, mix sizes, shapes, and heights. You might group all different round objects together as well as items with similar textures and colors.*

A stone pathway leads from the front to the back garden.

The living room is a visual treat with Nantucket artwork mixed with antique finds and family heirlooms; stained glass windows provide diffused winter light. The Victorian sofa holds needlepoint pillows made by the late Gwenn Gaillard of Opera House Restaurant fame and founder of the Opera House Cup race..

The dining room is perfect for cozy entertaining. Reggie says,
"Five people at most." A piece of pottery by Pierro Fenchi is a
prize possession from Reggie's Main St. Gallery days.

The little back sitting room serves as an office/library/study. It's a cocoon-like room surrounded by favorite books, a writing desk looking out over the garden.

33

Another small
room between the
living room and
back sitting room
holds more objects
of art: marionettes,
hanging glass,
French lanterns,
and more Pierro
Fenchi pots.

An American sleigh bed dominates the bedroom surrounded by paintings and curios on every wall. Everything from the warm brown pine floorboards, tapestry pillows, bed throws, rugs, and furniture exude a coziness born out of cherished surroundings.

"The roof sags on purpose," the owner said. While it has been restored inside, the exterior of the cottage looks much the way it did in the 1800s.

North Star

Greater Light, a historic building dating back to the eighteenth century, was once a barn for livestock. Two Quaker sisters bought and turned it into an art studio in the 1930s. Two other buildings were part of the property. One was called Lesser Light and the other, North Star, served as a carriage house. In 2004, former art gallery owner Lyn Walsh bought the charming North Star cottage that sits sideways at the end of the lane and employed her son to restore it. During the two-year renovation project, they kept making discoveries that changed their plans. They salvaged old wood and old plaster—even the beams were incorporated into the restoration of the building—and turned it into a charming, comfortable, art-filled cottage.

In 1850, what is now the living room was the entire building. There is now one bedroom and bath downstairs, another bedroom and bath on the second floor, and a spacious new "wart" (a Nantucket term for an addition) kitchen, designed to keep with its two-hundred-year-old legacy. "I went from a large house in Dionis to this small cottage, so I had to choose the things that mattered most to me," Walsh says. Her lifestyle is now much simpler than when she ran a gallery, and she enjoys the aesthetic paring down of her life, but admits it's a daily challenge.

Living in a small space makes one selective. A creative person knows how to devise space for storage and arrange furniture for optimum comfort and an aesthetic lifestyle. For Lyn, living with art and sculpture and interesting objects from around the world became the focal point of the interior design. Wherever she has lived, Lyn has surrounded herself with art and says, "I have a little bit of all the best artists that I represented and admired. Surrounding myself with art enriches my life."

Tips for Downsizing

Art collector Lyn Walsh offers tips for downsizing successfully:

1. *When furnishing from scratch, start with one piece and build from there.*
2. *You have to make choices. When it's between two items for one space, the one you love best, even if it doesn't match the sofa, wins out.*
3. *Live with each new item. Get used to it taking up room before continuing. Little by little, each piece you add will relate to each other.*
4. *Choose the items that have meaning for you, for example, the experience of discovering a certain artist. That's the piece you keep.*
5. *Be selective. If you don't have room for everything you love, store some things away and change out from time to time.*
6. *Make decorative objects useful whenever possible. Make food part of an artistic arrangement, like a bowl of fruit under a still-life painting.*
7. *Everyone has sentimental things they cannot live without. These are the things around which you can build a collection or arrangement.*
8. *Keep editing. Keep rearranging. Think of your home as a gallery; it doesn't have to remain stagnant, it can always be evolving.*

A small resting place at the top of the stairway holds a grouping of vessels, paintings, and sculpture. The master bedroom was decorated with selectively chosen paintings.

The living room was originally the carriage house built in 1850. The Japanese alter table holds three cubist women by Suzanne Green and underneath is a group of red lacquered vessels.

Light bouncing off the rose-colored furnishings gives the living room a rosy glow. Much of the subjects for Lyn's collections represent religious art and expressions of spirituality. The Madonna painting is by Karolina Danek.

41

The warm cherry wood kitchen is the hub of the house with all appliances at counter height. Everyday food products are stored in interesting containers. No commercial food labels are in sight. Apothecary jars hold dried goods.

Many pieces of furniture, like this dining table, came from a local auction.

The kitchen window looks out onto the border garden.

Steps and a brick path lead to the front door.

English Country

"When you've lived on boats," explains Pat David, "you learn how to conserve space." She and her Welsh husband, Jeremy, live in a three-room cottage right off Main Street. All the rooms open out to typical English-style gardens. In fact, if you stumbled onto this cottage in the countryside of England, perhaps in the Cotswalds, you wouldn't be surprised. The gardens, tended by Pat, exude a casualness that comes from knowing exactly what should be where. It all looks so natural and informal and integrated exquisitely, as though it has always been this way.

The owners, she the caretaker for the Old North Wharf cottages and he a caretaker for Nantucket's premiere houses, enjoy perfecting their nest as well as off-shore excursions on one of their boats when they have time.

When they bought the cottage more than twenty years ago, it was in terrible condition. They had to gut and rebuild most of it, giving them the opportunity to make it their own. Today it is shipshape with all sorts of clever cubbies and closets for storage, just as they had outfitted their boat for compact living. The architectural charm of the place is intact with modern lighting and new walls, a bathroom complete with a washer and dryer, and windows that look out on the natural beauty that surrounds them. At this elevation, it feels as though the building is a treehouse. It is hard to believe it's steps from Main Street.

A dining alcove off the open compact galley kitchen is below ground level at the front. Early beams add character to this bright space just inside the front door.

This intimate personal space was designed for comfort. Much of the furnishings are from England, Pat's heritage, although she grew up in Toronto. Persian rugs cover worn patina floorboards and the curved wall under the windows provides seating that might easily be found on a boat. Marine paintings, a ship model, and a carved shore bird reflect the couple's interest.

The small sitting area at the edge of the property is protected
by a rose trellis. The property is situated on a high elevation
overlooking trees below.

The bedroom opens onto a side patio and the lawn with the rose trellis. It is an aerie high above the town. There is storage in the bed platform.

The original
brick wall divides
the living room
and kitchen/
dining alcove.
A built-in wine
holder was
salvaged from an
island home and
fit perfectly.

A ledge around the below-street-
level living room holds nautical
accessories seen through the front
window. Roses grow over the trellis
and fill the facade.

The entryway is paved with stepping stones and a flower garden with roses and lavender, typical of the time in which the house was first built in the 1700s. The cobblestone driveway reflects the island's past.

Historic Restoration

The cottage was built in the 1700s by a chair maker and remained in the Christopher Swain family until 1906. The chair maker apparently wasn't overly concerned with accurate measurements, as this in-town house has a charming list to it. Over the years, the house settled so that doorways, floors, and walls all leaned this way and that. Being in the house was a bit like being on a ship. It was a mess with glass and cement in the yard, weeds taking over the place. Nothing had been done to it since the 1950s, and it would take someone with vision to see the potential. When Joan and Ed Lahey first saw it, Joan recalls, "It just spoke to us. I fell in love with the front room and the three tiny rooms, even the sloping bedroom with a fireplace. I could see beyond the weeds and broken glass."

But, even before the restoration work began, the couple lived in the house for a summer. "It was like camping out," Joan says, "but I was able to get a feel for the house." Working with local architect Chris Dallmus of Design Associates Inc., they designed the restoration and renovation that would include a downstairs bedroom and bath addition as well as a new kitchen.

The owners purposely avoided "fixing" the slant of the doorways or the uneven floors, as they felt it should be preserved. In fact, the floors tilted so badly that chair and sofa legs were reconfigured to compensate for the uneven floors. Having owned many early homes, including a sea captain's house on Orange Street, the Laheys know all about preservation and restoration and, when the house was finished, received a prestigious award from the Nantucket Preservation Trust.

But, as with many people who move into old houses, they are a family living in modern times, and so there are now new bathrooms and a spacious kitchen, elegant and crafted with care. The new master bedroom wing is so in scale with the rest of the house that it seems as though it could have been part of the original cottage. A balcony upstairs overlooks the kitchen and there are two more bedrooms and baths. There's also a living room, den, and dining area that seem to have been basically untouched.

Today the house sits nestled into the landscape and the completed restoration is proof of the homeowners' abilities to recognize the potential of a neglected home and to have the confidence to know that it would be worth the effort to restore it.

History of Sailors' Valentines

Sailors' Valentines originated by sailors aboard ships and were made with shells from Barbados, a regular stopping place for American whalers. The valentines were created in handmade octagonal wooden shadow boxes. The designs were created with a variety of shells glued in symmetrical rows, some more creatively arranged than others, depending on the skills of the sailor. They were intended to become gifts for the returning sailors to give to their loved ones and they also served the purpose of keeping the men busy during the long journey home. All the valentines we know of date from the early 1800s to the end of the nineteenth century. They are all made in boxes of the same wood, cedrela, or Spanish cedar. They all use the same shells and have similar designs. This last quality signifies that whoever created the first pattern became the example for all who followed.

There was enough space in back, off the new kitchen, for a patio. The fence around the property provides privacy where in-town houses were built close together. There's even room for a small koi pond in a corner of the property.

The new kitchen belies the age and cottage feel of the original house, but makes it complete for modern family living. Joan Lahey's exquisite replications of Sailors' Valentines are used in place of tiles under the kitchen cabinets. That's a cranberry scoop above the cabinets.

The homeowner
designed the floor
treatment in the
kitchen and chose tiles
to reflect the design.

A new master suite
was added within the
appropriate plot line.
Local artist Mellie
Cooper's handmade
paper painting hangs
above the bed. Wooden
window shutters
are typical of early
Nantucket homes.

The original wide pine floorboards in the dining and living rooms were painstakingly restored. The table is a family heirloom and creatively paired with molded Lucite chairs. An eclectic mix of art fills the walls and more of Joan's Sailors' Valentines can be seen in the living room beyond.

The cozy den with dark paneling (note the hidden cubby next to the painting) is the most used room in the house. As much of the original materials as possible were preserved.

The original back staircase winds from the old front hallway to the very slanted second floor. The thick, curved, plaster wall in the hallway curves around and leads into the den, probably called a parlor years ago.

The structure on the left was the original workshop turned into a one-room cottage. The new addition more than doubles the size.

The window treatment in the studio is made of elements that all came from yard sales. Surprisingly, the custom-made valances perfectly fit the studio windows.

An Artist's Abode

In the mid-1900s, an island builder constructed a workshop on a little in-town lane. He later converted it into a one-bedroom, one-bath cottage before selling it to a well-known island artist. She loved its quaint charm and throughout the years they worked together to design and double its size to include three bedrooms, two baths, a living room, and kitchen plus a separate post-and-beam barn-like studio on the property.

When furnishing the cottage, the goal was to keep the maintenance low and to decorate around the artist's paintings so the house would always have the flavor of a Nantucket artist's cottage. The artist also wanted her home to reflect her Swedish background. The country kitchen with open shelves, a twelve-foot window seat, and details like latch door handles, pine wood doors, and big beams in the new master bedroom are cottage-style details. The artist's paintings of hydrangeas and seascapes are filled with blues, and they define the interior design of the house.

Furnishing a comfortable and stylish home on a small budget takes a lot of planning. Toward this end, we began with a floor plan, a color scheme, and the IKEA catalog. We started with the few pieces she already owned—mismatched folk art dining chairs, a color scheme she loved, two wicker chairs, and a table found at a yard sale. The old living room would become a casual family room with new cushions for the wicker chairs covered in the same fabric used on the window seat. A few throw pillows in blue and white tied all the furniture together. A new cover for a lounge chair was made from the leftover remnants.

IKEA is known for good design at very reasonable prices and much of the furniture is made of light wood, perfect for the house and a Swedish feeling. Their fabric and curtains are also of good value, and careful shopping can yield a variety of simple, Swedish-style lamps for different purposes. Two Thomas Woodward blue woven area rugs soften the painted white floors. Wide floorboards are often painted white in Swedish homes. Throughout the house, small antique family accessories combine with the more modern pieces. Using folk art chairs, for example, around an IKEA table with simple hanging lamps lends character to the dining alcove. A tall, painted mirror fits perfectly between the windows, creating the illusion of a wall of windows. An artist friend's painting on the wall adds significance as a reminder of Nantucket's early art scene.

Tips for Decorating on a Budget

The trick to furnishing a house with inexpensive pieces of furniture is to choose carefully. Buy the basic large pieces and fill in with small antiques or traditional accessories that elevate the lesser pieces. The following are some tips and tricks.

1. *Begin with a floor plan and include windows and door openings. Add measurements to every wall as well as areas beneath windows.*
2. *Make a list of the basic items needed for each room.*
3. *Work with catalogs or online sites and write down the measurements of every item you intend to purchase so it will fit exactly where you want to use it. Draw the items to scale on your floor plan.*
4. *Choose a color scheme and determine how you will use the colors whether in the fabrics, paint on the walls, curtains, as accessories, paintings, rugs, chinaware, and bed linens. Sometimes an arrangement of silk flowers can provide the necessary touch of color.*
5. *A word of warning: IKEA furniture comes unassembled (that's part of the cost savings), but it is designed to fit together perfectly. If time is a factor, consider this.*
6. *When it comes to fabric, new is better. If you buy secondhand chairs, for example, new cushions will update them. Spray paint is a good way to refurbish old pieces and always use white for summer homes.*
7. *Sheer curtains are lovely in the summertime, but shutters are a nice alternative for a cottage feel. They need less maintenance and provide air and privacy control.*
8. *Always buy good mattresses even if the bed frame is inexpensive. This is a purchase you will never regret. The same goes for the linens, towels, quilts, and especially the pillows. Buy the best you can afford. Cotton quilts on guest beds are practical and look great.*
9. *Lighting is important but doesn't have to be expensive. Get the right size base and shade.*
10. *For a summer home, area carpets win out over wall-to-wall. If someone spills something on a cotton carpet, it can always be cleaned easily.*
11. *Use all white chinaware. Always buy at least a dozen of everything for the inevitable breakage.*
12. *Once you have the basic furniture in place in each room, you can have fun adding whimsical, interesting, important, and meaningful accessories—but remember, the more you fill a room, the less maintenance-free it will be.*

Sheer ready-made curtains allow light to pour into the family room and soften the windows. A built-in window seat has storage underneath for storing the artist's prints. The wicker chairs and coffee table are yard sale finds. The open kitchen is a real country gem with blue-and-white checked curtains for a Swedish touch. Open shelves hold blue and white dishes.

The IKEA dining table in the alcove seats eight comfortably with mismatched folk art chairs and a Kilim rug for character. The hanging lamps are from IKEA and the mirror between the windows came from an island store. Donn Russell's print fills one wall with a watercolor painting by Barbara van Winkelen on the opposite side: a nod to the early Nantucket art colony.

The living room is part of the new addition with more of the artist's paintings. The coffee table is from IKEA, the slipper chairs from the Nantucket Lightship Basket Museum yard sale opposite a newly purchased sofa.

The master bedroom is part of the new addition with its own full bath. It was designed with the same country feeling as the original part. High ceiling and exposed beams, wide pine floorboards, a patch-work quilt, and an antique chest are reflective of the simplicity of the Quaker era on Nantucket.

The open floor plan includes this country kitchen. All that was needed was a fresh coat of paint on the cabinets, walls, and floor. No above counter cabinets, only open shelves are used with a closet as a food pantry.

The post-and-beam barn-like studio was turned into a delightful one-room guest cottage with a full bath and sleeping loft. It is separated from the house by a privacy hedge.

A circular garden fills the property between the main cottage and the studio. A variety of perennials and summer annuals fill the grounds, which are completely enclosed with growth, providing a visual and noise barrier from the busy in-town street.

The small, compact kitchen is fashioned from pine boards. A collection of lightship baskets lines the bench

Self-Expression

Like so many cottages on Nantucket, this one needed a great deal of work when the artist, Donn Russell, bought it almost forty years ago. Russell and his lifelong friend Arthur Schaefer shaped the house and gardens into a personal expression of their individual talents.

The house is a reminder of how Nantucket used to be when it was a haven for artists whose first creative expressions were evidenced in their living spaces. Every area of every room is a visual treat. Found objects discovered on beachcombing forays, weathered wood, and driftwood have been incorporated into the structure of the house. Mixed with Donn's sculptures, paintings, and handmade pieces of furniture, the look is functional and eclectic. Early Persian and Oriental rugs brought from travels around the world add to the balance and proportion of the furnishings, contributing bright spots of color to the worn-patinaed, wide, pine floorboards.

The cottage comprises a small entryway that leads directly into the galley-like kitchen with plenty of clever storage space to make it functional. Weathered gray boards made into cabinet doors and an old porcelain sink provide character. A small dining area open to the kitchen houses a table built to the right size for the room.

Two upstairs bedrooms and just one bathroom downstairs complete the house. Very little has been done to modernize this home, as the owners felt that too much has changed over the years on Nantucket. The houses have gotten bigger, more lavish, and less personal. The old-fashioned charm of these old houses has been lost, and the owners took pride in keeping its basic qualities intact.

This half-acre property is large, by in-town standards. Seen from the windows, the greenery, with all sorts of indigenous trees and bushes, provides a natural barrier from the busy street beyond the garden gate. Once inside the property, the Zen-like quality takes over. The grounds are filled with a concentric garden of flowering plants and shrubs that evolved over many years. Rose bushes, peonies, tulips, and daffodils come back every year and whatever looks good at the farm stands is added. In this way, the garden reflects the seasons.

Arthur's passion for gardening is evidenced in the garden that fills the property. Occasionally it has been on the Nantucket House and Garden Tour, a much-anticipated annual event that raises money for charitable island causes. While the garden may have a formal look, the best thing about it is its lack of formal planning. It is a garden that, like the cottage, evolved through loving care over a period of time.

Planning a Cottage Garden

Small houses require gardens that are in scale with the house. Several different gardens lend themselves to this situation. The following are some suggestions for in-town gardens.

1. *A cottage border garden of farmhouse hollyhocks along a fence is always pleasing.*
2. *An herb garden lining a walkway appeals to all the senses.*
3. *Low seasonal plants in flower boxes or movable pots are practical.*
4. *Wildflowers provide a cutting garden.*
5. *Pick a color or type of plant and overdo it in a small area. Incorporate rocks and found objects like driftwood in the garden.*
6. *Create an enclosed and defined area with bricks or a low bamboo fence and fill it with appropriate flowers for the season.*
7. *For all-season blooms, choose plants that bloom early in the season, later in the summer, and those that come out in the fall. It's easiest to do this in a small confined space.*
8. *The concentric garden in the middle of this yard surrounds a large urn filled with topiary and seasonal flowers as the centerpiece. A small concrete garden seat breaks up the arrangement, adding interest and providing a place to reflect or simply rest when weeding.*
9. *Create drama with a path of paving stones or bricks from the house to the garden, setting the stage leading to the grand event.*

Colorful rugs create a patchwork pattern over the worn pine floor. The coffee table was made from a lobster trap. The yellow metal sculpture in front of the fireplace was created in 1980 by Michael John Jerry. Lion sculpture by Donn Russell, sprial wood sculpture by Chad Whitlock, and painting over the sofa by George Murphy.

Reclaimed floorboards and weathered driftwood were used on the ceiling and to make the divider screen. Pine is a common wood used on the interiors of early cottages. The painting is called Two Bluefish *by Sterling Mulbry, an artist who showed at the Main Street Gallery in the 1980s.*

A little meditation garden is filled with all varieties of green shrubs, trees, and plants directly off the kitchen.

A brick path leads from the studio to the cottage with little off-shoot pathways that lead to tucked away areas along the path. The statue is four feet tall and is a copy of one in a chateau in Southern France. The property is lush with greenery, interesting rock formations, statues, and planters that contribute to the park-like setting.

Nantucket Window Boxes

Window boxes are a Nantucket staple. We see them on in-town houses and cottages and under shop windows along Main Street and side streets in town. They are especially prevalent on the wharf cottages along the piers jutting out into the harbor and the whale cottages in the town of Siasconset. When the Quakers settled in town, they were dedicated to plainness. The buildings were unadorned with weathered, gray shingles and white trim, just as they are today. If there was a garden, it was strictly to grow herbs and vegetables for cooking and confined to small spaces. Over time, the desire to have some color, if only temporarily, after the long gray winter, yielded small pocket gardens and sometimes a row of hollyhocks along picket fences. No one is quite sure of the exact date of the first window box, but this was a good solution to containing a garden and sprucing up the fronts of houses if only for the short season. Today, the window boxes all over town are a source of pride with store and homeowners and the subject of many photographs taken by visitors to the island. At times, it almost seems as though there is an unspoken competition to see who can create the best-looking window box.

Old North Wharf cottages side by side in full summer regalia.

Old North Wharf

Old North Wharf is Nantucket's second oldest wharf, built in 1750. It juts out into Nantucket Harbor and is lined on both sides with modest structures originally built as fishing shacks and boat shops. In the early 1900s, these shacks were used to cull and prepare quahogs to be shipped to the mainland. This was where the serious business of the fisherman's world was carried out.

Each building was named after a whale ship, all once owned by Jared Coffin. The wharf was designated a historic district in 1955. Throughout the years, many of these buildings were sold and transformed into charming little houses, which the current owners refer to as boathouses.

During the season from mid June until mid-September, these cottages are surrounded with small gardens, window boxes, and pots brimming with native flowers. It's an easy walk from Main Street to Old North Wharf, an extension, really, of the core shopping district but miles away in terms of seclusion. The comings and goings of the steamships and private boats is the main attraction and there is always a breeze coming off the water. Strolling here on a summer afternoon is one of the delightful detours for locals and visitors alike.

The Wharf Rat Club is one of the more famous and iconic of the North Wharf cottages. The club was founded in 1915. It was originally a general store where men sat around a potbellied stove and traded island stories. The club has no bylaws, dues, or membership. Acceptance is based on the ability to tell a good story.

The cottages of Old North Wharf sit on stilts in the boat basin. The gold dome of the Unitarian Universalist Church is seen in the distance.

This two-story cottage, Essex, has all the amenities of an in-town, larger home with one extra advantage: the water all around. The double boathouse doors are part of the original architecture.

The bedroom doors open to a balcony that juts out into Nantucket Harbor where the sounds and smells of island life are part of living. Carefully chosen furnishings for comfort and style turn a once rustic structure into a place of simple luxury.

Essex

Essex is one of the larger boathouses on Old North Wharf with two floors and an upstairs balcony. While some of these cottages were painted bright white to make them feel more spacious, this one was renovated in an updated boathouse style with pine walls, floors, and ceilings. The heavy rafters also add to the boathouse feel of the place. But the main attraction is the water all around. Every door opens onto that spectacular view and reminds the owners that they are living on an island thirty miles out to sea.

The ceiling, open to the rafters, gives the room a feeling of spaciousness. Pine boards placed horizontally over the walls and ceiling and wide pine floorboards give the interior the boathouse feeling.

This cottage sits at the end of the wharf in the Boat Basin.

Even a boathouse deserves a Nantucket windowbox.

Peru

Peru sits perched at the very end of the wharf. It is bolted to sturdy pilings and sits on high stilts. Even so, during a Nor'easter, being inside this little boathouse must be quite an adventure. The little over one thousand square feet has been designed as efficiently as the inside of a boat cabin with all the details and amenities afforded a modern inland cottage. Rustic has been replaced with comfort and twenty-first-century style.

Living on the water, almost in the water, can be a challenge. Each time the homeowners visit their summer getaway, they are reminded that life along this wharf is subject to change depending on the weather and storms that can have an effect on their little boathouse.

But this is what so attracts them. They see Brant Point Lighthouse at the entrance to the harbor. They watch the ferryboats carrying visitors to and from the island and they relish their perch at the center of harbor activities.

Like others you'll meet throughout this book who live in small cottages, these homeowners are mindful of limited space, careful not to clutter or overpower the rooms. The furnishings they chose are related to a nautical connection with lanterns, marine paintings, nautical chart fabric on the dining room chairs, and touches of blue in dishtowels, dishes, painted kitchen chairs, and, of course, bunches of bright blue hydrangeas.

The water is a constant panorama outside every window.

The open Dutch door lets the boat basin and all its activities be part of the interior. It's like living on a houseboat, without the constant motion.

The kitchen is small and efficient. A Claire Murray rug with its nautical scene adds warmth and a nautical touch to the wide pine boards.

The oval dining table sits in a niche created with a closet to the left and bookcases to the right. A hooked rug fills the space between the windows. Since the cottages are practically touching one another on the wharf, simple Roman shades provide privacy.

East of George

This summer cottage sits on pilings right in Nantucket Harbor on Old North Wharf, and the sound of the lapping waters under the house is part of everyday life. The homeowners' little runabout is tied up to the dock next to their deck, always ready for a quick getaway to Coatue or Tuckernuck for a picnic.

The boathouse, called East of George, is accessed from the shell footpath of Old North Wharf and started out as a small rope locker in the 1920s. It has had just three owners. A trellis fence covered with roses and pots of flowers provide privacy around the front deck where there is a little seating area. The front doors are original to the boathouse and painted bright blue. The interior is an open room with sliding barn-like doors across the back that lead to a deck overlooking the harbor. The all white painted interior brightens the space. The exposed rafters and wall studs, open ceiling, and many of the details contribute to the boat-like feeling

While it's small, the living room can accommodate a crowd without feeling cramped. There are plenty of intimate seating areas—on the deck in front and on the deck facing the water in the back. Heat from the fireplace takes the chill off the room in the shoulder seasons and on chilly summer nights.

A new kitchen was created with attention to boat-like details. This wonderful makeover within the main room adds to the enjoyment of cooking dinner for friends. Every square inch is utilized just as one might do on a boat. Storage for everything was carefully and creatively planned in the kitchen, including a little cubby behind a door just big enough to hold a lobster pot.

The upstairs contains a master bedroom and two bunk bedrooms for the grandchildren. Shelves covered with curtains serve as closets in each bedroom. Trunks hold blankets and toys, and clothes are hung on wall pegs. Baskets are also used for storage. People who live in small spaces become masters of ingenuity.

Much of the furnishings came from island antique shops and auctions. Details abound with family treasures mixed with island arts and crafts like old decoys, carved shorebirds, lightship baskets, ivory, and scrimshaw—much of it by some of the best artisans on the island: Nancy Chase, Nat Plank, Susan Ottison, David Hostetler—and totally unexpected in a wharf cottage, adding to its character.

Decorating Tips for Flexible Living

Small spaces demand that everything have a purpose. How does one do this without succumbing to a cluttered look?

1. *Choose upholstered furniture that doesn't overpower the room, but is comfortable. Use wooden pull-up chairs for extra seating when needed.*
2. *The dining table might have an extra leaf to enlarge when needed rather than be oversized all the time.*
3. *Beware of sharp edges. An oval table is graceful in a room and is practical when navigating between the table and the sofa on a regular basis.*
4. *Create small areas within the larger space for different activities. For example, a round table can also be used as a desk. The chairs around it can be used as the extra dining chairs when the main table is extended.*
5. *Many decorators think family photos should be displayed in designated areas like the bedroom or bathroom. Grouping them on one small table or wall can give comfort without detracting from the overall decor.*
6. *Eliminate clutter on kitchen countertops and find interesting ways to keep much used items at your fingertips.*
7. *Take advantage of small, narrow wall spaces to mount a creative container or spice rack.*
8. *You can have a lavish garden even in a small outdoor area. Movable containers, window boxes, and exterior plant holders add cottage charm. Bunch small herb plants in an interesting container.*
9. *Cover open shelves with a curtain or a lightweight quilt hung over a curtain rod. Use wall pegs for hanging clothes, summer hats, umbrellas, etc.*
10. *Overdo a good thing, but be sure each thing is good.*
11. *Following the nautical theme of the boathouse, miniature lightship baskets filled with seasonal flowers create the centerpiece for the dining table. Fresh flowers are lovely on the kitchen counter seen from the living room.*
12. *If you have a vacation home, keep it simple so it remains a vacation home away from home.*

The boathouse sits on pilings thirty inches above sea level. Decks on the first and second floor overlook Nantucket Harbor.

There is no compromise to comfort in the living room. Upholstered chairs and a full-sized sofa, plenty of occasional tables, and an intimate eating area surround the fireplace. Island crafts infuse the space with character appropriate to the building's history.

The kitchen has a boat-like feeling created with stained fir boards, ship's knees, and lots of hidden storage. The front door opens to the deck where pots of herbs await the cook.

The fireplace provides the main heating source and charmingly slants to the right. The relief carving over the fireplace is a funky piece that came from the side of an Italian wheelbarrow. Miniature lightship baskets, ivory carvings, a ship's model, and carved shorebirds adorn the brick mantelpiece.

Continuing the boat theme, a thick boat rope serves as a stairway banister to the second f125loor. Two small guest bedrooms carry out the nautical theme with red, white, and blue quilts. Pegs on the walls and open shelves provide storage. Rainbow fleet models are lined up on the wall ledge open to the rafters.

Twin beds carry the red,
white, and blue theme in the
second tiny guest bedroom.

Cottage Gardens

A cottage garden is a distinct style of garden that uses an informal design, often dense plantings and traditional materials. It is never grand or formal, but rather casual, with a mixture of ornamental and edible plants. When we think of a cottage garden, we might imagine a little structure in the English countryside and, in fact, this is its origin.

In the 1870s in England, they were primarily made of vegetables, herbs, and fruit trees. It might have been enclosed with a rose-covered arbor. They were intended as cutting gardens and the plantings were chosen for their use or scents. Over time, even large estate gardens had a smaller section called cottage gardens. On Nantucket, roses were planted as a cottage garden staple, giving off their rich scents at the beginning and midsummer growing seasons. Modern-day cottage gardens include regional perennials with lush foliage and fragrance, along with annuals and free-climbing plants associated with cottage gardens of the past. The best examples of cottage gardens on Nantucket are on small areas around in-town houses and in the little village of Siasconset, where the roses grow up the sides and over the rooftops of the little whale cottages.

Today, cottage-style gardens are created around houses of all sizes with the simple formula: an informal look and a seemingly casual mix of flowers, herbs, and vegetables. They often have useful paths or hedges designed to look artless, as though everything in it has just grown there by accident, rather than contrived. Plantings are usually dense to avoid the need for excessive watering and weeding. Stone pathways imperfectly laid out with curves and irregularities might be included.

Tips for Planning Nantucket Cottage-Style Gardens

1. *Choose plantings for their old-fashioned appeal.*
2. *Arbors give a casual appearance.*
3. *Something old can lend an air of charm.*
4. *Use native plants and those adapted to the local climate.*
5. *Plant roses, climbing roses in particular.*
6. *Cottage garden flowers include: lavender, hollyhocks, carnations, sweet William, marigolds, lilies, peonies, evening primrose, daisies, lily-of-the-valley, and cowslips.*
7. *Herbs with household uses: lavender, sweet woodruff, thyme, sage, basil, parsley, catnip, and soapwort.*
8. *Typical fruits might be raspberries, apples for cider, and pear trees. A modern garden might include a dogwood or crab apple tree.*

Irregular stones create a garden path with densely planted perennials on both sides.

A lawn filled with wildflowers is a typical cottage-style garden.

How to Grow Hydrangeas

Growing Hydrangeas

The beautiful large hydrangea bushes are a Nantucket garden favorite. They are perfect no matter where they are planted; as a frame around a garden, delineating a yard, peeking through white picket fences, or as decorative bushes on either sides of our front entryways. They have also become a favorite flower for island weddings. Visitors to Nantucket always remark about these flowers and ask, "What makes them so blue?"

According to Craig Beni, owner and operator of Surfing Hydrangea Nursery on Somerset Road, the color is affected by the relative acidity of the soil. Agents such as aluminum or iron will usually produce a bright blue color, so we can assume that Nantucket soil gets all the credit. If you add aluminum to the soil they can go from pink to blue. An alkaline soil will produce flowers more pink. The genus *Hydrangea* is comprised of a tremendous assortment of subspecies, cultivars, and varieties. The cool maritime climate of Nantucket provides excellent growing conditions for most of these.

While there are hundreds of varieties, two types of hydrangeas are most prevalent in home gardens and landscapes on Nantucket. One is the bushy *Mophead,* producing the most beautiful arrangements filling lightship baskets on most Nantucket tables in the summer. The *Mophead* resembles pom-poms with their large, globe-like blooms. You see them all over the island and in August when they are the fullest they are spectacular. The other is the *Lacecap* that has flat petals, is more delicate, and the blossoms are not as full and therefore not as dramatic. They have a center of female seed capsules surrounded by larger male blossoms.

Another type of hydrangea seen on the island is the *paniculata* that need several hours of sun to do well. It is the only type of hydrangea that can be pruned into a tree form. This hydrangea is often white and is somewhat cone shaped rather than ball shaped. The best-known paniculata is *PeeGee* (paniculata grandiflora).

Cultivating Hydrangeas

The hydrangea is a hearty shrub that thrives in sandy soil and doesn't need much fertilization. Another contributing factor to its lush beauty is our moist foggy air.

This ornamental shrub begins to bloom in early July and lasts for six to eight weeks. By the end of summer the colors begin to fade and the blossoms become brittle. Their color changes and they go into what is referred to as their "antique" stage. They are then appreciated in a different way.

Many Nantucketers use the dried blossoms to make holiday wreaths. Others simply enjoy them in an arrangement. In this way the lovely flowering shrub continues to give us pleasure.

Pruning Hydrangeas

To keep hydrangeas full, once planted, they need regular pruning or they become leggy and saggy. Hillary Nowell and Pete Smith of Bartlett's Farm say it's really important to know the species and cultivars of the hydrangeas you are growing. The ubiquitous *Nikko Blue* hydrangea blooms on the previous season's growth. If you prune off those branches in spring, you won't get any flowers that season. If you need to prune for shape, prune before the end of summer. However, the old-fashioned tree hydrangea, *PeeGee* blooms on new growth so you can prune after it begins to grow in the spring. Many of the newer varieties of *H. macrophylla* like *Endless Summer* bloom on new and old growth, so you can prune them anytime. Be sure you know which ones you have, so they can be pruned at the right time for maximum flowers every year.

Tips for Rooting Cuttings from the American Hydrangea Society

1. *Cut a branch of the hydrangea shrub about 5 inches long. For best results cut from a branch that did not flower this year.*
2. *Remove lower leaves.*
3. *Cut the largest leaves down to half their size.*
4. *Insert the cutting into damp vermiculite, sand, or other clean material.*
5. *Water well and allow to drain. Keep the soil moist but not soaking wet. Cover the cutting and pot with plastic and, if possible, keep plastic away from the leaves, perhaps with sticks. They should "take" in two to three weeks.*
6. *Cuttings don't do well through the winter. Start them in early summer for the best chance of survival.*
7. *Hydrangeas grow best if they are fertilized once or twice in the summer. A fast release fertilizer like 10-10-10 works just fine. Don't fertilize after August.*

At one end of the rill, an arbor holds a garden swing for contemplating part of the garden. This garden owner's advice: "Every vista needs a structure at the end."

110

A gravel path lined with a shrub border of boxwood, Enkianthus, and hydrangeas leads from the back of the house to the garden. Greenery of different heights creates interest along the way.

In-Town Gardens

In-town gardens have more shelter, so plantings can be less hardy than out of town. Space affects the style of a garden. With limited space, the design can be more orderly. A sloping property lends itself to a two-level plan.

Before planning this garden, the owner studied hundreds of garden books and was influenced by the gardens she saw in England, France, Italy, and especially Scotland, where the soil and weather is similar to ours.

Once all the grass was removed, the ground was covered with gravel to keep the weeds at bay. For easy maintenance, the plan included lots of boxwood and other green shrubs. While the garden is made of perennials, there are pots of annuals strategically placed around the deck and patio areas for color and excitement. There's an abundance of *Euphorbias*, ideal for borders, and *Kniphofia*, which bloom in late spring and produces large blossoms all summer long.

A stonewall delineates the two levels. The lower level is the real garden and any flowering plants on the upper level are mostly white. There are areas for sitting and contemplating. A wonderful pear tree in the middle of the upper level seems to anchor the whole backyard. Found objects are strategically placed for interest and an element of surprise.

Every garden requires water, and one of the more interesting features is the rill, which is a narrow, maybe six-inch-wide trench about six to eight inches deep "planted" so that it intersects and divides the lower level of the garden. Water runs down the rill into a basin and returns via a simple pump that recirculates and provides a constant trickling sound. The Arabs created rills in the desert, where the sound of trickling water was important to them. Rows of snaking boxwoods curve along each side of the rill, creating a pattern around which flowering plants and grasses have been staggered by height, shape, and color. The scents, sounds, and filtered sunlight create an in-town oasis. Quite simply, a garden nurtures and adds much to the aesthetic and spiritual quality of life.

Allium is the Latin word for "garlic," and this flowering plant is of the onion genus. The flowers vary in color depending on the species. They like sunny areas.

Gardening Tips

1. *Look through many garden books and magazines to get ideas about the kind of garden that appeals to you.*
2. *Make sketches of what you'd like the garden to look like.*
3. *Consider your lifestyle and how the garden will be used. Do you have children and a need for a play area? Do you want a place to barbecue? A place for contemplation? Casual versus formal?*
4. *A good rule of thumb for hardscaping: don't mix materials. Use all brick or gravel or stone in a particular area such as pathways or walls.*
5. *Have a loose plan for the framework of your garden and then be a little daring.*
6. *If you have a long vista, put something at the end to punctuate it, such as a structure, a tree, a hanging swing, or a statue.*
7. *Create interest by mixing up your plants and flowers with different shapes, colors, and heights.*
8. *Plant what will survive best in your area. Deer and rabbits will find your garden. Learn what plants will deter them and what they don't like to eat.*
9. *Consider maintenance and how much time you want to devote to tending your garden. Some plantings require lots of watering, for example.*
10. *Stagger your plants so you have blooming flowers from spring through fall. Another kind of garden might contain all green bushes and shrubs and lots of grasses.*
11. *Design a water feature. A small fountain on the side of the house or fence might be enough.*
12. *Look for unrelated objects such as a weathered shutter or door, a stone statue, or a garden stool to incorporate into the garden.*

A rill is a shallow trench-like structure that enables water to circulate in a steady stream that runs through the garden. The water empties into a basin and then returns. Flowering plants fill spaces between the boxwoods.

A variety of roses in a variety of colors growing up the side of a cottage.

Marking the Seasons

Nantucket is known for its gardens, but it is the roses, hydrangeas, and daffodils that get the most praise. In fact, the season kicks off with the Daffodil Weekend Celebration heralding the arrival of spring. We even have a parade featuring more than a hundred vintage automobiles decorated with daffodils. These well-preserved antique cars are owned by islanders and off-islanders, many of whom bring them over on the ferry for this event. There are tailgate picnics along the route from town to Siasconset on the Milestone Road where, many years ago, the Nantucket Garden Club members planted more than a million daffodil bulbs.

In June, the roses nudge out the daffodils for center stage and literally take over the place. They grow in profusion in gardens and up trellises on the fronts of cottages and over the rooftops. In fact, the roses are so full that the gray-shingled cottages in the tiny village of Siasconset is a sight out of a fairy-tale book. And just when we think they're gone until next season, they surprise us with another blossoming season in August. Sometimes we have a variety of colors from pale to shocking pink as well as yellow.

But it is the bright blue hydrangea blossoms that capture everyone's attention. Many years ago, the beautiful large hydrangea bushes literally edged out the roses for "favorite flower" status on Nantucket. Maybe it's their spectacular blue color (even though there are white and pink blossoms as well), or perhaps it's a combination of the bright green leaves and the shape of the bushes. They are perfect no matter where they are planted; as a frame around a garden, delineating a yard, peeking through white picket fences, or as decorative bushes on either sides of our front entryways. They have also become a favorite flower for island weddings. Visitors to Nantucket always remark about these flowers and ask, "What makes them so blue?" There has been lots of speculation, but the popular opinion is that we just have the right acidity in the soil and our climate is perfect for growing the most spectacular blossoms in the country, maybe the world. You be the judge.

A single rose marks the summer season.

Roses, roses, and roses.

One of many hydrangea species found on the island.

Daffodils by the Old Mill.

Roses and hydrangeas are often used together.

White and blue hydrangeas in mid-summer bloom.

Old North Wharf cottages surrounded by hydrangea bushes.

Only the white hydrangea can be pruned into a cone shape.

Ivy Lodge built in 1780.

Roses grow over the trellised rooftops of these early whale cottages.

The Village of Siasconset

The little village of Siasconset, at the east end of the island, had a modest beginning as a group of one-room fishing shacks. While the first of these shacks, Auld Lang Syne, was thought to have been built in 1675, it wasn't until the mid-1800s that 'Sconset, as it is familiarly called, became a popular place for whaling captains and their crews to ease into island life when they weren't quite ready for bustling downtown Nantucket. These one-room shacks, with cooking done outside, offered simplicity to life that appealed to the men. But then the women visited and, of course, spruced up in the way of "warts," or tiny bedrooms not much bigger than a ship's cabin. A porch, actually, a crude kitchen came next. Since it was most impractical to bring wood from town, these additions were constructed from a mixture of cast-off materials. Wood from a torn down boathouse or a storage shed was commonly used. The pump in the town square served the cottages though they all had cisterns, little slate sinks, and hand pumps as well as coal stoves in the kitchen. Some of these little shacks were used as a general store, a post office, or a teahouse. Shununga, one of the best preserved cottages with the original section dating back to 1680, was a tavern run by the original owner, Betsey Cary, and in 1873 it became a post office.

When the town of Nantucket became popular as a summer resort, 'Sconset was discovered and soon earned a reputation as an art colony with many actors, artists, writers, and musicians coming to stay and perform at the 'Sconset Casino.

Today the village of 'Sconset is pretty much the way it was. The sides of the in-town streets are lined with the charming, low, slant-roofed, shingled cottages. The little yards are open to the street and roses grow up and over the rooftops.

Many of the little whale cottages have remained in the same families for generations. Villagers appreciate the quaintness of the place and the isolation from the summer activities in the town of Nantucket. The village is quite self-sustained with a market, post office, package store, a little café, and a takeout restaurant for lunches under a shade tree on the porch—all clustered around the village square. Both the Chanticleer Restaurant with its lovely, low-key garden setting and The Summer House overlooking the beach provide elegant, sophisticated meals for discerning tastes.

But it is the little cottages along Broadway (so named not for the theater but because it was the broadest path leading into town), Center and Front Streets—and the cottages of and around The Summer House—that gives this eastern end of the island it's overwhelming charm.

Longtime residents of 'Sconset often reminisce about their childhood summers here and now offer this experience to their children and grandchildren. They describe sun-filled days of endless summers to do nothing but swim, read books on rainy days, and look up at a clear star-studded sky at night. They savor a sense of peace, fresh air, the scent of wild roses, and the ever-present, rhythmic sound of the surf. It is a world unto itself during the summer months.

Roses and hollyhocks are found in cottage gardens.

126

Built-in seating around the living room was fashioned after a childhood family boathouse. Nautical touches include the lighting and weathered, wooden fish sculpture.

None Too Big

The name says it all! This iconic 'Sconset cottage in the Pump Square section of the village has a colorful history. Built in the 1700s, it is believed to have been moved to its current site from Sankaty Light. In the 1860s, it was home to the lighthouse keeper of Sankaty Head Lighthouse. It later became the Burgess General Market. At one time, a whale boat was stored on the first floor.

It was an abandoned trash heap when it was purchased in 1987, and, with the help of local architect Gwenn Thorsen, the couple that bought it did extensive restoration and redesign. Many additions have altered the structure and nothing original remains except a little buttery underneath the house.

The objective of the homeowners was to maintain the authenticity of the house as much as possible. Because all three of them had built boats, they decided the interior would be designed for the efficient use of space. It would be neat and organized and shipshape, with lots of built-ins, like the bunk beds reminiscent of a family boathouse. They followed their excellent instincts with impressive results.

The cottage sits sideways on the lot (see page 126) and one enters through a gate under an arched trellis. It has the old-fashioned charm of an English cottage garden filled with perennials and boxwood nestles right up against the house. Some of the unexpected details include the gently curving border crested with clusters of stones gathered from Coatue—the arm of the island that juts out into the harbor—and the irregular stone steps embedded with seashells, leading to the front door. Avid gardeners, the homeowners planned the gardens as carefully as they designed the house. They called on their knowledge of gardens in the English countryside and planted appropriate flowers and shrubs in keeping with the scale of the house and the village of 'Sconset. Much loving care has gone into this garden over the years, as storms and weather have taken a toll. But each year the garden design provides a new creative challenge that these homeowners are more than ready to take on.

The small paned antique windows on the potting shed were brought here from the Cotswolds. Window boxes brim with flowers and fleece vine that grows up the trellised side and over the roof in uninhibited profusion.

Back in the 1800s, a two-story addition was built across the gable end of the cottage. That side now comprises the downstairs kitchen and the second-floor living room, reached by a circular, custom-designed stairway. The pine galley table was once part of an old Norwegian clipper ship.

The owners combined boxwood and colorful flowering plants at the entrance of the house. Potted plants lead up the stone steps to the front door.

A center hallway leads to a guest bedroom and a back stairway to the master bedroom suite. A painted floorcloth with a fish design echoes the boathouse theme.

The blue-and-white seashore theme is carried throughout the house. The walls of the guest bedroom are covered with white beadboard like the rest of the house. Simple lace curtains afford in-town privacy without blocking out the light.

The combination of white beadboard walls, pickled floors,
scrubbed pine furniture (mostly
Danish), and the use of a white
canvas with touches of blue gives
the house a clean, fresh feeling. The
beehive fireplace was added to the
upstairs living room.

A little side door leads into what is now the bedroom. Flowers bloom all around this 1760s cottage.

Dexioma

The name of this cottage, built in 1780 on Broadway, means "Welcome" in Greek. It has been called "the most perfect gem" by Henry Chandlee Forman, an architectural historian and the author of *Early Nantucket and Its Whale Houses.* The south end of the cottage is the oldest section while a north kitchen was added in the early nineteenth century. By the late 1840s, "warts" were added to either ends and an early boathouse was attached along the Front Street side. The kitchen window and little back patio enclosure provide a clear view of the ocean. The two gentlemen who occupy this early whale cottage are no strangers to historic homes, having previously lived in an early home in Bucks County, Pennsylvania. Michael May is the executive director of the Nantucket Preservation Trust and Housley Carr is a journalist who specializes in writing about energy. They appreciate that they are becoming part of the history of this historic cottage.

The house tilts so much that being in the bedroom can lead to vertigo, but one has to marvel over the fact that it is still standing, having been built more than two hundred years ago and without the benefit of modern materials and skills. This cottage, like the others in this part of the village, was unplanned and haphazardly built. Nothing seems to be aligned. Mary Williams, who owns several early cottages in the Underhill Settlement in the village of 'Sconset, designed and planned the restoration, mostly confined to making the kitchen functional. You cannot tell what is new and what was original, as the new parts were made to look old.

Housley says, "The best part of this house is the indoor/outdoor living." The double kitchen doors open onto the back sitting area where tourists and neighbors stop for conversation as they pass by on the shell path that divides the rows of close-knit houses. All summer long, roses and clematis grow up trellises, some onto rooftops. Michael says, "This house is such a wonderful example of architectural preservation and how the houses evolved over time."

While the cottage was once used only as temporary shelter, with a fireplace for cooking and heating, it seems to be made of tiny rooms that evolved into multiple uses over time. However, there is one large bedroom with a fireplace and built-in storage, a small bathroom, and another tiny guest room as well as the living room and new kitchen, the largest room in the house.

The "wart" is laden with roses and the back patio, off the shell path, affords a clear view of the ocean.

Roses grow up and over the roof of one of the earliest whale cottages, Dexioma, in the village of 'Sconset. The picket fence contains the cottage garden filled with roses, lilies, and hollyhocks.

The renovated new kitchen addition blends seamlessly with the early part of the house. Reclaimed shutters, wide painted boards on the walls and ceiling, reproduction bureau drawer pulls, and original wide floorboards reflect the era in which the cottage was built. Modern appliances make it all work.

The rafters in the new kitchen give it a spacious feeling and provide storage space for scalloping racks and nets. Double doors open wide to expand the living area to the patio overlooking the ocean.

A built-in corner cupboard in the bed-room is typical of these cottages. A small bathroom has been upgraded.

Built-in drawers reflect an efficient use of space. The wood surrounding the fireplace is original to the cottage. A narrow door, probably the original front door leading into what was once the living room, opens onto the front deck.

The living area, off the kitchen, is simply furnished. A folk art painting over the sofa was found in a Pennsylvania antique shop.

A dry sink is built into a narrow space in the front entryway.

The front door was relocated from the side of the house so that a new kitchen addition could be created to the right side of the house.

This 'Sconset cottage bears a quarterboard with its name, Tuck't Inn, over the kitchen window. Window boxes filled with pink impatiens and a border of hydrangea bushes add to the country charm.

Tuck't Inn

The name of this cottage says it all. It is tucked away from the street in the heart of the village. The original owner, an engineer with an artistic bent, was a collector of maritime antiques who made reproductions of harpoons and ships' heads and had done some good things with the cottage. Built in the 1950s, the structure wasn't one of the early whale cottages, but it had similarities and the same charm—and the lot was large enough to create a new kitchen and a bath above it for the existing second-floor loft bedroom. To their credit, the homeowners retained the original paneling, floorboards, the cobblestone fireplace, large antique beams, the narrow stairway complete with a ship's desk against the stair wall, and the open loft area above the living room.

They added little things without detracting from the cottage feel: new hardware on closet doors, shutters on the windows, and storage created in the upstairs bathroom. Every bit of space has been used efficiently for scaled-down living with plenty of storage in unexpected places. Relocating the front door, once on the side of the property, "made a big difference to the facade," the homeowner says. Now there is an inviting front porch, a Dutch door that opens into a small hallway leading into the living room, and the kitchen is nicely situated to one side of the house. Windows were replaced with French doors along the back wall of the living room to brighten the interior. The room now opens onto a beautifully manicured lawn and patio filled with containers of flowers.

In the front, roses grow up the trellis to the rooftop and window boxes overflow with pink, summertime impatiens. This is truly quintessential Nantucket cottage style. The best features of the original house have been emphasized and integrated well with the improvements. The interior does not feel dark, as the paneling might suggest, nor is it cramped, due to the openness and change of ceiling heights. For example, the living room is open to the rooftop and loft bedroom, while an intimate dining alcove under the loft suggests a separate room without walls.

The cool blue-and-white color scheme offsets the warmth of the worn wood and is perfect for a cottage by the sea. The furnishings are comfortable and scaled appropriately for the space and the nautical artwork—most by island artists, some from Maine—maintains the flavor of a long ago era associated with Siasconset and its surrounding dwellings.

Furnishing a small cottage should be carefully planned to make the most of the space. The following are some suggestions:

1. *Make every piece of furniture count; it should have a purpose.*
2. *Surprisingly, a few large pieces will be more comfortable and look better than lots of small pieces.*
3. *One color scheme throughout will make the house seem more spacious rather than choppy when you go from room to room. The color scheme can carry over to bedding and bath towels as well. When a guest opens the bathroom closet in the new bathroom, the shelves should be stocked with matching blue-and-white striped towels.*
4. *Look for every little area that can be used for storage; for example, dead space can often be found under a stairway. Cut a door into the space and use it as a utility closet. A window seat offers compact seating with storage underneath.*
5. *As you can see from this 'Sconset cottage, everything doesn't have to be painted white. The warmth of the wood paneling, beams, and floorboards adds to the coziness and early Nantucket feeling. Use a light or neutral color for the upholstered furniture.*
6. *Lighting is important. When you have high ceilings, low table lamps make the living area inviting and intimate.*
7. *Choose furniture that can be used in different ways; for example, the dining area is perfect for the cottage. Two extra chairs placed on either side of a side table under the window can be pulled up to the table for guests.*
8. *When adding on or renovating a kitchen, for example, keep it in the style of the rest of the house. A large, modern granite and steel kitchen would not fit with the style of this small-scale cottage.*
9. *A small house needs editing at all times, as it will look best when neat and pared down.*
10. *As with all the other furnishings, art and accessories should reflect the size and style of the house. If it's an early Nantucket cottage, even when renovated, it can be an unexpected surprise to find objects that reflect the island's history.*

The original paneling, floorboards, and beams add character and warmth to the downstairs living area. Variations in ceiling height create different living spaces. The master bedroom is straight ahead at the front of the house.

Many nautical artifacts and paintings associated with Nantucket's whaling days grace the wood-paneled wall above the cobblestone fireplace. The wall extends to the roofline, creating an open and spacious feeling in the living room. Whale carvings were made by Michael Bacle.

A dining alcove was created under the loft bedroom. The cutout in the wall allows light to spill in from the entryway and kitchen beyond and serves a practical purpose as well. This dining space can accommodate six to eight people with a bench on one side of the table and pull-up chairs on the other.

The original stairway leads to a sleeping loft and the new bathroom.

The loft bedroom is open to the living room. Red and white quilts, blue quilted pillow shams, and nautical paintings are perfectly suited to the folk art decor. The beds were part of the original furnishings in the cottage.

The newly renovated kitchen was designed appropriately for the house with a surprising mixture of updated appliances and cabinets, but with an old-fashioned cottage feeling. The paint color is Benjamin Moor Abbington Putty.

An upstairs bathroom was added over the kitchen. There are four closets in this room with plenty of storage for linens and towels.

Container plants and simple weathered furniture is perfect where there is an ever-changing view of the harbor below the bluff. Flowers grow up the trellised side of this outdoor living room.

Gardener Amy Manning created a perfectly delightful cottage garden filled with roses, lilies, and delphiniums in reds and pinks and bordered with cobblestones and a picket fence. Hydrangea bushes (a Nantucket staple) border the deck. Outside, decks surround the house with plenty of space to enjoy the landscape.

On the Bluff

If you could conjure up the perfect setting on the most perfect island for a most peaceful getaway from busy Manhattan island, you couldn't do better than the cottage on the bluff overlooking the Atlantic Ocean in the village of 'Sconset. Hidden from the road and accessed only by a path of wooden steps lined with the sweet scents of native wildflowers, the journey there is rivaled only by the spectacular views unveiled once you reach your destination. Nestled into the dunes, the cottage is unexpectedly modern, with large glass windows that allow the indoors and outdoors to blend seamlessly.

Years of life on the oceanfront had taken its toll on the cottage, but with the help of many talented people and the input from the island's Conservation Commission, the cottage was transformed into this exquisite retreat. Trudy Dujardin of Dujardin Design Associates and Price Connors worked with their clients, two Manhattan doctors, to turn this house into a comfortable and stylish retreat.

As often happens when renovating these small cottages where expanding or adding on to the original structure is not an option, taking out walls, raising the ceilings, and reconfiguring the use of the space makes them seem more spacious, both visually and in feeling. Builders Hatch and Burns are credited with the impeccable craftsmanship throughout this project.

Trudy Dujardin, who has clients all over the country, applied her signature blue, white, and cream-colored palette to reflect the colors of beach, ocean, and sky, creating a serene backdrop for artwork and a sprinkling of the couple's antiques throughout the cottage. The understated elegance of the interior design has been purposely orchestrated so as not to detract from the views and the landscape, making them an integral part of it.

A nautical theme runs through each room with a framed early map of Nantucket on the walls and stripes, crabs, and starfish fabrics on the sofa and chairs.

A clear view from the front deck through to the ocean.

INN DA BLUFF

A milk-painted early folk art cabinet, lightship basket, and hooked rug on the wall add character to the modern interior.

A custom-made sofa in the living room, handmade chairs in the kitchen, a round Amish rug on the wall, and the rounded molding are just a few of the custom designs found throughout the cottage.

The wall slats in the guest bedroom are painted a seafoam blue to reflect the color of the ocean.

The design firm created custom lighting fixtures for the home and used reproductions of antique nautical lamps to reflect Nantucket history.

The little cottages sit side by side with their low-slung rooflines and charming architectural details.

Underhill Cottages

In 1879, Edward Fitch Underhill discovered Nantucket and became a major developer here. He built a cluster of small, low-roofed, shingled, basic one-room summer dwellings (with ladders leading to sleeping lofts for children) to imitate the whale cottages on Broadway and Center and Front Streets. This little enclave of cottages, known as the Underhill Settlement, was built on three streets behind The Summer House Restaurant.

The local firm of Angus McCleod Designs recently renovated four of these cottages at numbers 9, 12, 14, and 15 Pochick Avenue, for which they received the prestigious Historical Renovation Award for design from the Nantucket Preservation Trust. The Trust deemed the work, completed by the firm and the homeowners, along with the skillful assistance of carpenters Bill Willet and Bernie Civitarese, an example of how additions to historic buildings can be accomplished while maintaining the integrity, sense of scale, and proportion of the original structures. The cottage renovations were done with extreme sensitivity to the early streetscape of Underhill's original designs.

Pochick Avenue, with its mere shell path of a street, is lined with the original Underhill cottages, most of which have been responsibly renovated by Angus McCleod Designs.

This cottage was renovated by Angus MacLeod Designs in 2007. The second story "wart" on the left is the loft bedroom. In the 1800s, a floor was typically laid over two bedrooms below, creating a cramped attic space with a little door opening reached by a ladder from the main room. They were called hanging lofts. Similar structures were built in Wales at the time.

The new kitchen and dining area addition looks as though it has always been part of the cottage. The slanted roof is covered with painted pine boards like the rest of the house. The chandelier seems so right for this space. It's liberating to accessorize a cottage. Anything goes, and Angus and Deb take pleasure in salvaging and repurposing, whether it's their choices of building materials or the interior furnishings.

Main Top

Deb and Angus MacLeod are an award-winning architectural and interior design team. They are dedicated preservationists, not only in house renovation, but also in the way they live. They are a couple true to their belief that "creating sacred spaces is our passion." For the past twenty years, they have been based primarily on Nantucket and in Boston. Their work on the cottages along Pochick Avenue in 'Sconset has earned Angus MacLeod Designs the prestigious Historical Renovation Award, well deserved for bringing a level of quality craftsmanship to all their projects.

They are very proud of the work they've done on these early cottages, working with outstanding craftsmen/ builders and like-minded homeowners who care about preservation. When we arrived to photograph Main Top, the home they are currently living in (they caretake the houses they have restored), they were on their way to their Saturday morning ritual, yard saling. "We love to recycle good things from Nantucket homes," Deb explained with enthusiasm, showing us the crocheted covers she reclaimed and arduously restored to use as chair covers in the living room. Deb and Angus are devoted to furnishing the cottages in keeping with their original intent of living simply. The interiors are as important to them as the architectural restoration and renovation.

This cottage at number 9 was much smaller when it was built in 1885. Deb and Angus, along with their longtime friend and homeowner Harriet Johnson, renovated the cottage for Harriet's children in 2007. A new kitchen/dining "wart" was added as well as a hallway with a bathroom that connects to a new bedroom carved out of what was once a shed. While the rooms are small, Angus's talent is designing furniture that has dual purposes and creating storage that it is integrated into minimal space. Deb and Angus take pride in the details they have incorporated into these cottages to add to their specialness, reinterpreting their enchanting qualities that go hand-in-hand with the lifestyle that has always been embraced in this part of the island. Edward Underhill had a good idea, and Deb and Angus MacLeod are improving on it. They understand the elegance of simplicity and luxury without excess.

The cottage to the left and the shed to the right were attached with a hallway, creating a sweet little enclosed patio area with hydrangea bushes and flowers growing up the facade. Twig and wicker furniture and pillows covered in vintage fabric found at yard sales maintain the cottage style. The dark green trim is also a typically approved color.

Underhill built these cottages with one room and a sleeping loft for children. The MacLeods modernized the interiors, insulating them for year-round living and reconfiguring the use of the rooms. An ample entryway with its open ceiling to the rafters leads to the living room. The all-white interior makes it fresh and bright and the antique pieces of furniture are in scale with the rooms.

The living room is filled with comfortable chairs covered with reclaimed crochet coverlets. The built-in sofa, with storage below, opens into a full-sized bed when needed. Lace napkins and table covers are used as café curtains, casually hung with old-fashioned, wooden clothespins.

The new hallway has a bathroom to the left. The gracefully curved doorways, another MacLeod Design signature, provide a subtle, unexpected and elegant detail.

Quarter Deck

Quarter Deck, another cottage across the street, is one of Angus MacLeod Design projects. It, too, was once owned by longtime and much loved resident Harriet Johnson. The bay window on the side is a dining area.

There's a living room, dining alcove, kitchen, bedroom barely big enough for a double bed, bathroom, and a screened-in porch in this whale cottage. The restoration work included creating a loft space, perfect for kids, as there's barely enough height to stand erect. The furniture reflects the era of its origin, and the artwork goes with the redesign. It's an interesting balance between the old and the new.

Deserted beaches are easy to find in all directions.

A rose-covered cottage on the way to Polpis.

Out-of-Town Cottages

Much of the island is conservation property.

*Springtime at
Children's Beach.*

*View of Hither Creek from
a Madaket deck.*

Great surfing at Cisco Beach.

The best place to watch the sun set is in the fishing village of Madaket.

This *We'll Always Have Paris* plaque was a first anniversary gift from Stacey to Peter to commemorate their honeymoon. The stepping stone path winds through the daisies and up to the arbor.

Old boat buoys hang from the outdoor shower wall and the side porch holds an assortment of birdhouses and potted plants.

Living with Heirlooms

The cottage out on Polpis Road, quite removed from town, was built in the 1800s. For many years, it was inhabited by the late Mac Dixon, famed for his role as director of the Nantucket Theatre Workshop. The most recent occupants, Peter Greenhalgh, sales manager for the Joyce and Seward Johnson Gallery at the Artists Association of Nantucket, and his wife, Stacey Stuart, special events manager at the Nantucket Historical Association, enjoy the serene oasis they have created away from the energetic environment of town and their work.

When one has amassed a collection from several generations of family, it is both a responsibility and a challenge. But Greenhalgh has always derived pleasure in surrounding himself with the treasured heirlooms he inherited from his ancestors, who came from England and Scotland. He takes comfort in living with the past. "It isn't a burden to take care of these things," he comments, "but rather a joy. When I arrange a group of silver items, for example, I remember seeing them in my family home and it evokes pleasant memories."

When he married Stacey a few years ago, the cottage was already crammed with several generations' worth of Peter's possessions, brought with him from many moves. The couple has managed to incorporate their family collections, appreciate things of quality, and decorate with items that remind them of a gentler time. This early cottage and everything in it pays respect to another era, one that is revered on Nantucket.

Peter built the arbor with college friends. Everything planted here is typically found in a cottage garden, many of which came from friends. Informal furniture and garden sculptures are also considered cottage garden staples.

The grandfather's clock commands an imposing place in the parlor, which is what they called living rooms in early houses. It is dated 1802, from Wapping, England, and was owned by Peter's grandfather and inherited from his mother's family. The prism lamp was converted from a whale oil lamp.

The porch is a favorite place for breakfast and lunch. In winter, the sun is low, bathing the room in sunlight. Vintage fabric lends old-fashioned charm.

A builder renovated a small cottage, added a front porch, and landscaped with native plants.

Ship Shape

Jay Hanley, an island builder and owner of Blue Star Contruction LLC, says he bought a rather ordinary seven-hundred-square-foot cottage on a fairly large lot and turned it into a modern compact dwelling. Realizing he would have to gut the inside, he began with an outline of the floor plan and then basically divided the space in half, one part for private space and the other for a kitchen/living room combination, or the public areas. Even when building larger homes, he encourages his clients to design a small, intimate, private area used strictly by the family with plenty of public spaces for sharing and entertaining. Having worked with many architects and clients, this builder/homeowner has been exposed to many different designs and sized houses. He finds small spaces the most fun because they are the most challenging.

When it came to his own house he says, "I was going for an urban, nautical feel." The look he has created is without any pretentiousness. Every detail has been addressed.

The materials used on the interior of the house came from a dismantled barn in New England and were re-milled and used on the floors. Distressed ceiling beams were used as the collar ties. The walls and ceiling are covered with painted poplar shiplapped horizontally. The only furniture that isn't built-in is a sectional sofa that creates an ell around a leather ottoman used as a coffee table. One wall of the living room is all built in bookshelves with storage drawers beneath. A ship's ladder fits neatly between the bookcases against the living room wall and is used to access a storage loft over the private areas. Even in this space, there is storage under the low eaves with doors that latch up on the sloped ceiling.

The house feels more spacious than its square footage would imply due to the high ceilings and flood of natural light. There is a bank of windows along the front and side of the living room and a small window in each gable end of the house just under the roofline. French doors in the kitchen open onto a flagstone patio surrounded by a garden and storage shed.

No matter the size of your house, this builder says it's important to find an intimate area. That's the key to making a house welcoming and putting people at ease. When it comes to a small space, Jay says that a good carpenter can do anything with wood. In the end, it comes down to thinking outside the box and realizing that it can be shaped to utilize any space you have. When beginning a project, he tries to get everyone involved—the architect, the builder, and the client—to make sure everything is feasible from a cost-and-design perspective. "Like any decent business, teamwork creates a successful end product," he says.

Tips for Building or Renovating a Small House

Jay Hanley, owner of Blue Star Construction LLC, offers the following advice to those building a small house or renovating an existing space.

1. *Create a good team that can work together. If you have an architect, he or she might recommend a contractor the firm has experience working with. If you do this at the inception of the project, you will avoid a disjointed process.*
2. *Listen to the professionals to make sure everything is feasible from a cost-and-design perspective. This will always save you money in the end.*
3. *Consider the best way to take advantage of the site.*
4. *Think on paper before you even consult an architect. In other words, make a list of what you want in your home. Once you have plans, consider the furnishings and adjust the placement of windows and doors or work around them. The more detailed your plans in the early stages, before anyone picks up a hammer, the more successful and cost efficient the project will be.*
5. *Plan to have a "signature" room. This is an intimate space for family only. This is key to feeling comfortable in your own home.*
6. *Identify as many details in the design phase as possible.*
7. *Meet with the architect, builder, even the subcontractors before the project gets underway.*
8. *Listen to the professionals and take advantage of their knowledge and experience.*
9. *When planning the landscaping, try to use indigenous materials and be realistic about what sorts of plants and bushes will do well in your area and on your particular property. Jay's garden is filled with a variety that grows in all seasons. The window boxes are filled with very wispy grasses that can be seen from all the living room windows and create interest from inside.*
10. *Like any decent business, teamwork creates a successful end product. A good building plan executed with everyone on the same page will work for anyone creating a home no matter how large or small, whether from scratch or as a makeover.*

A sleeping loft provides room for an occasional overnight guest while the hallway leads to Jay's bedroom and bath—the private area of the house. There's a small powder room on one side of the hallway and a washer and dryer in the closet to the right.

The open living room faces the kitchen. The stainless steel appliances are top-of-the-line, countertops are mahogany, as are the floors. Off-white painted cabinets have oil-rubbed, bronze pulls and the porcelain sink is a reproduction of those found in early New England farmhouses. French doors lead to the garden.

Not having a toilet in the master bath allowed the owner to fit a small powder room in the hallway. The walls of this room are covered with grass cloth paper and it is elegantly appointed. A washer and dryer are neatly tucked into a closet opposite the powder room.

The bedroom is just ten by ten feet. The platform of the bed includes drawers for clothing and there's an open walk-in closet on the opposite wall. French doors lead to a side patio with a hot tub and outdoor shower. The lamps on either sides of the bed are modeled after those that once lit Parisian workshops with a pendant that can be easily raised or lowered because it is weighted for counterbalance.

A new wide deck with a massive fireplace surrounds the house. The lawn and beach grasses beyond add to the feeling of spaciousness and privacy even though neighboring houses are a stone's throw away.

Surfside

Surfside, on the south shore, is one of the most popular island beaches and an easy bike ride from town. Simple cottages still remain along the bluff overlooking the beach, although erosion on this side of the island has resulted in the loss of many of them over the years. To downsize their lives, one couple decided to refurbish an old cottage to get a new/old cottage. Toward this end, they hired the architectural firm Botticelli and Pohl of Nantucket. It was important to them that the building materials and the design of the house reflect the characteristics of the early Nantucket beach cottages. When you create a new/old house, you have the opportunity to keep the feeling of the old while incorporating a bit of luxury not found in old structures, such as up-to-date plumbing fixtures, a new kitchen and bathroom, efficient windows, and other practical considerations. What they achieved is a simple design, deliberately sparse with exposed beams, vaulted framing, and a feeling that suggests carefree living. There is a straight-forward approach to this structure, with no fancy moldings or anything to suggest a grander home.

What infuses this house with youthfulness is the all-white interior, painted furniture, rattan sofas, woven rugs, blue fabrics, and a collection of sea-worn bottles in cobalt blue and sea foam green. This cottage isn't furnished with castoffs the way rustic cottages from the past might have been. It is skillfully decorated to invoke that same casual feeling, but with comfort and low-key elegance. The luxury in this house is in its simplicity.

The floor plan consists of one large room with a brick fireplace, original to the house. To create continuity, the bricks were covered with the same painted white board used throughout the house. All the doors are extra wide and passageways ample, further enhancing the feeling of a luxurious cottage for modern living with a nod to retro Nantucket cottage style. When you recreate space, you can design things to simplify the rooms, such as a window seat in the bedroom to eliminate the need for freestanding furniture, while adding the sort of charming detail often found in older homes. For all its modern conveniences and lovely furnishings, the house has all the nostalgic qualities of an old-fashioned cottage, only better.

Tips for Renovating in the Nantucket Style

1. *Research houses typical to the area where you will be building or renovating.*
2. *Consult with a local architect so he or she can advise you about what can and cannot be done on Nantucket and help with the Historic District Commission approval process.*
3. *Consider using materials that are indigenous to the area; for example, early homes on Nantucket often used soapstone for countertops. This is used in this Surfside cottage. Beadboard was often a staple in cottages.*
4. *If it's a vacation home, make it as compact and streamlined as possible. The grander the space, the less carefree your vacation time will be.*
5. *Consider your lifestyle and how you will use the house before meeting with an architect.*
6. *Create a file of tear sheets of houses, colors, textures, fabrics, furniture, etc., that you can share with your architect so together you can create a plan that will result in a successful project.*
7. *Step it up a notch: it's all in the details! Well-designed fixtures such as lighting, kitchen and bathroom faucets, tubs, appliances, and sinks make a new/old house luxurious, elegant, and functional. Waterworks products were used in the Surfside cottage bathroom.*
8. *Many manufacturers of bathroom accessories offer reproductions of early styles and, while they aren't antiques, they have the look and often function much better. The Kohler Company, for example, makes a steeping tub that has the look of an early claw-foot tub.*

The sun porch is a new addition and doubles the living space. The land-scaping, appropriate to the area, was created by the 'Sconset Gardener. Borders of Rosa rugosa bushes bloom all summer and are appropriate for a beachside site.

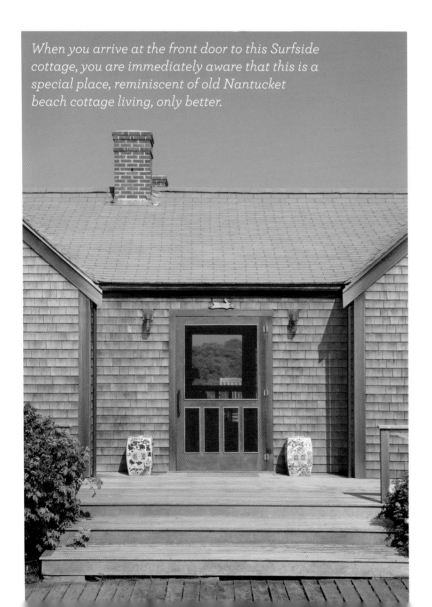

When you arrive at the front door to this Surfside cottage, you are immediately aware that this is a special place, reminiscent of old Nantucket beach cottage living, only better.

The view, looking out from the front door, is always spectacular even when the fog rolls in.

The open studs create a summer camp feeling. The old brick of the fireplace was covered with the painted wallboards and the brick surround was painted white as well. Closets and a small guest room fit compactly off one end of the living room. The painting is by local artist Illya Kagan.

French doors from the living room open into the sunroom. This new addition with hinged windows faces toward the ocean. The furnishings continue the rattan and blue-and-white theme with more cobalt blue bottles lining the rafters.

A reproduction soaking tub is reminiscent of early claw-foot tubs and this niche in the bathroom was created exactly to size. Open studs provide little cubbies for essentials at hand, just the way you might have stored them in your camp bunk.

The country modern kitchen is open to the rest of the house with cabinets for easy access, a large porcelain sink, soapstone countertops, and two unexpected chandeliers like those that once held candles.

The outdoor deck areas double the size of the living space indoors. The cottage sits in the middle of an acre of land surrounded by mature plantings. Simple herb gardens grow around the base of the trees on the property.

Old-fashioned weathered Adirondack chairs face the pond where Greg often takes a break from painting to fish.

Polpis

Six miles east of Nantucket town and bordering the inner harbor is the area known as Polpis. It's partly surrounded by the inland waterway, a peninsula that breaks up the harbor. When the island was first settled, the Wauwinet tribe of Indians occupied this area. Over time, this gently rolling landscape was made up mainly of farms. During the 1800s, Polpis was a flourishing village, and in the early 1900s, three summer cottages were built by off-islanders and a permanent road was built through to 'Sconset. Many speculated that this beautiful section of the island would change and there would be much travel this way. In reality, Polpis changed from a bustling village to a quiet little settlement that seems far from the real action that takes place in Nantucket town.

An acre of land may not seem expansive, but on Nantucket it affords the space and privacy an artist might crave. For more than twenty years, Greg Hill (who signs his paintings G.S. Hill) and his wife, Judy, have lived where we might call "way out there." Surrounded by mature trees, a pond fed from an underground spring two hundred yards away (the pond is home to an endangered spotted turtle), and what appear to be rolling hills, there isn't another house in sight. Every window of the cottage has a view of nature. "I claimed the third bedroom for my studio and added sliding doors that give me the best views of the expansive lawn and trees. We cleared out much of this area," Greg says. The property, owned by the Corkish family for several generations, held four summer cottages, all with the same footprint. Convinced that the Hills would preserve the land as it was and always has been, the owners sold Greg and Judy the cottage they had been renting for twenty years.

Built in the early 1970s, they didn't change the basic feeling of it. The kitchen was remodeled, slightly, and they added on a deck and a small, second bathroom. The cottage is one thousand square feet, but there is just as much space outdoors, doubling the living area in the summer months.

The cottage was insulated and reverse shiplap was placed horizontally on the walls. The knotty pine trim throughout and pine ceilings add to the cottage feeling. As avid appreciators of island crafts, the couple has an impressive collection of Nantucket lightship baskets. Paintings by local artists both past and present fill the walls of the cottage. As a longtime member of the Artist's Association of Nantucket, Greg's work is represented there as well as the G.S. Hill Gallery on Straight Wharf in Nantucket Harbor.

Nantucket Lightship Baskets

Lightship baskets are one of Nantucket's indigenous crafts. They were originally made on board the South Shoal lightship. These baskets were made of a tightly woven cane with white oak staves or ribs and an oak rim around the top, an oak handle, and a wooden bottom. This type of basket dates from at least the mid-1800s when molds were first brought onto the lightship. By the 1860s, a considerable number of baskets had been made.

Nantucket lightship purses were introduced in 1945 by a weaver named Jose Reyes who moved to the island from the Philippines. He called his creation a "friendship basket." It had a wooden lid over an oval basket and quickly became the most fashionable accessory carried by island women. You may notice them as you walk around the island today.

The cottage is filled with antique lightship baskets as well as those made by local craftsmen Paul Willer, Rich Leone, Maggie Silva, Dan Bursch, and Maggie McCluskey. The subject of the painting to the left of the back door is of old-time Nantucket character, Brownie, by John Strope.

The small dining area and kitchen to the left open onto the deck where there is a fire pit for dining on chilly island evenings. The walls of the house are filled with a rare watercolor by Robert Stark and paintings by local artists, including John Lochtefeld, Bobby Frazier, David Lazarus, Donn Russell, Barabara Van Winkelen, and many others.

A small, third bedroom was converted into Greg's studio where there are views from every window. Artist's proofs on the counter and a painting on the easel will be ready for a gallery show.

The little "wart" (a Nantucket term for an addition) to the right is the guest cottage part of the early sheep shearing barn. The dog is real, the sheep is not.

Painted white beadboard walls, beams, and horizontal ceiling boards, white kitchen cabinets, and pine floorboards with touches of blue are quintessential Nantucket country cottage treatment.

A guest bedroom has storage under the platform. Slated wood walls are typical treatment in a cottage.

Madaket Sheep Barn

In the 1800s, the area on Madaket Road across from Sanford Farm was sheep-grazing country and a major part of the island economy. It was covered with huckleberry, bearberry, and golden heather. The shearing pens were located just east of Miacomet Pond. At that time, there were as many as 12,000 sheep on the island. In mid-June, the sheep were brought there from various areas over the island and washed in the pond before shearing. It was a three-day celebration.

This farmland was ultimately divided and developed and today a main house sits high on this acre of land. The barn was kept intact, however, and is the first thing you see as you turn up the driveway off Madaket Road. For many years, it was a carpenter's workshop, but the current owners renovated half of it for a guest cottage, leaving the other half to house bicycles and tools and such. The barn-like feeling was incorporated into the renovation and the owners take great delight in sprinkling the lawn with many statues of sheep in all different poses. From afar, this land looks just as it did when the real sheep were left to graze freely.

It's a simple structure with an open living space, a small and efficient kitchen, a bedroom, and a bath. Painted all white, except for the pine floors, the cottage is furnished in a Nantucket-favorite cottage theme of blue and white. It is a casual style designed for easy maintenance and carefree summer living. The garden is simply hydrangea bushes planted around the cottage side of the barn. The wind blows across this high elevation even on the hottest August day.

This Quidnet cottage is just steps from the beach.

The couple can lie in bed and look out at the pond.

Quidnet

On the north side of Sesachacha Pond is a section of the island known as Quidnet, meaning "at the point." It was settled around the same time as Siasconset. There is nothing there but a quiet beach and summer homes and the peaceful surroundings of nature and the sweet sea air.

This quiet area of the island proved to be the ideal location for a perfect getaway for a busy couple who own The Summer House Inn and Restaurant in 'Sconset. This Quidnet cottage, just steps from the beach, was once a fishing shack with a wood-burning stove. When this couple filed for permission to enlarge the cottage, they had to stick with the existing footprint. So they made it an architectural feat with glass walls, doors opening to the outdoors from all the rooms, and space-saving furniture like armoires for closets. The homeowners decorated it with a casual, eclectic, yet elegant English country style. Everything in the house was custom-made, gleaned from their many travels and working with experienced craftspeople. There are only two bedrooms, but the glass walls provide the illusion of space, as does the open, gourmet kitchen. The outside of the cottage was as carefully planned as the interior with such thoughtful amenities as a large deck off the bathroom that includes an outdoor shower with a roof over it. When you step out of the bathroom door, you can take a shower in luxury—outdoors.

For this gourmet kitchen, the homeowners shipped pine woodwork in pieces to Nantucket from England. The wood was retrofitted around the appliances.

The two sinks in the bathroom were dropped into a pine cabinet.

The fireplace surround in the living room is from a British home. The coffee table was reconfigured from a dining table.